SOCIAL MEDIA MARKETING

Table of Contents

INTRODUCTION

Currently, social media marketing is the most powerful tool that can help businesses to reach customers and prospects (whether small or not). But with over 88 percent of all companies selling on at least one social media platform, you can see how tempting it can be for the company to get lost in all that noise.

To achieve more organic visibility, meet committed brand fans, and even generate more sales and leads on your company social media pages, you'll need a succinct marketing strategy to rise to the top. Thankfully, this book offers just that for you.

The book will show you how to promote your brand on social media, peeling through the layers of the most popular social media sites to get to the heart of what makes an online marketing campaign effective.

Whether you are either active on social media or have never had a Facebook account, this book will lead your social media marketing campaign every step of the way—through building your account and improving your profile, to posting content that your audience will want to connect with, and the different ways to advertising and promoting your brand for more views and followers.

We will look at Facebook, YouTube, Instagram and Twitter, in this book and show you that given the fierce competition, social media marketing can be effective in your business.

A strong presence on social media is something that the company can't afford to miss. Continue reading to see how to create a plan that will bring thousands of followers to your profile   instantly.

CHAPTER 1

THE IMPORTANCE OF SOCIAL MEDIA

You have heard definitely heard the word 'social media' unless you've been living under a rock. You probably have an active account one of the popular social media sites. I am not going to go into describing social media for the sake of your time or confuse you with its early rise. Let's look at why social media is so important and how its success can be taken advantage of.

Asides from connecting with friends and family easily and conveniently, social media offers many other benefits that people couldn't enjoy in the past. Social media has become an integral part of today's modern society, including getting to know people from all over the world, keeping up-to-date with the latest news, expressing your thoughts, and discovering new items, goods, and services.

The social networks are one of the fastest growing industries in the world, rising with an insanely fast pace. There is no question that many organizations take advantage of the social media activity and manage to increase their conversion.

You can't be more wrong if you think about social media as nothing but a phenomenon that's destined to fade away. With more and more people joining each day and successfully use social media platforms for different purposes, it is easy to say that the social media sector is certainly at its height and will only grow bigger in the coming years.

Forget about magazines or TV ads if you want your company to grow, because right now, social media is the way to broaden your business.

STATISTICS DON'T LIE

If I have not yet managed to convince you that selling your business on the most popular social media sites is the best business practice for your product/service today, then perhaps these numbers can shed some light on you and make you understand that the best way to reach your target audience is to promote your business on social media.

As of 2019, the world today has 7.7 billion people. It's interesting to know that 4.2 billion of these people are internet users, but the fact that more than 2.7 billion internet users are active on social media is even more fascinating. This ensures that more than 64 percent of internet surfers are on social media at any time on effectively. In reality, the average time people spend on social media is nearly 2 hours, or more accurately, 117 minutes, according to many studies done over the past few years. This is the reason why most of the small businesses that are active on social media post daily. Since statistics also say that there is a new user of social media virtually every 10 seconds, it is quite obvious why it can turn out to be highly profitable to sign up for some social media activity.

Why Your Business Needs Social Media?

Not being on social media at this stage is like searching through a telephone book to find your hairdresser's address. Or still in possession of a Nokia 3310. And while there's nothing wrong with using a two-decade-old model of cell phone or doing it old-school with hand-written telephone books, one thing is certain—certain people miss out on the benefits of the technology of today. And that's all right, if you're just a guy with a philosophy of no-modern-technology. But if you're a company looking for a way to improve the conversion and get as many incentives as possible, it's a must to be online.

Social media is the internet for many people, and they waste their hours scrolling down their social media. Why? There is no reason to leave. The social networks basically have it all, from talking with friends to being up-to-date with events, searching and purchasing products and services. If you want the business to succeed, it is of vital importance to have a solid social media presence.

If your business is not still active on social media, this is definitely the missing link that can reinforce the connection between your product/service and your clients. Still not sure if the time and effort are worth it? Here are the benefits of being on the different social networks:

Web Traffic
Marketing your business on the different social media is a key part for your web traffic:
Posting on Social Media Pushes Your Targeted Audience
When people surf the internet for related products/services, you want your company to be the first thing people will see. But if you're not active online, is that really possible? Posting on social media on a regular basis will help you conquer the first search page, which in turn will increase your earnings.

To order to increase web traffic, these social media posts are extremely valuable. Think of what happens when you redesign your website, for example. With the search engines, it certainly takes a while to get momentum, right? It means that there will be small number of customers who will be aware of your new content. Posting on social media will help your prospective customers quickly find their new content and then guide them to your website. This means you don't have to wait until a client clicks on your website to find out about your updates. Social media allows you to meet potential customers even if they don't want to shop at the exact time.
Social Media Posts Boosts the SEO

—

8

For your online presence and overall market, search engine optimization is of great importance. Don't be misled that it doesn't matter that much. SEO experts know which places are traffic-free and which lies alone and overlooked. Clearly, a great content campaign will spike your search rankings, but social media posts can also bring more traffic to your web. You can quickly customize your website by re-sharing popular content and encourage current and future customers to take a peek. The boosted traffic would result in inbound clicks and will have a major impact on your Google rankings popularity.

Quoting Can Make You More Reachable

A quick quote can sometimes bring more traffic your way. Whether you've used a PR tool like HARO to locate experts for your website or just want to quote an expert with a strong influence on social media, this can certainly help your business. Chances are that person will most likely retweet or re-tweet your post by citing (and tagging!) an authority on your tweet or Facebook post that will help you reach potential customers from their list of followers and increase traffic on your web.

Connecting with Customers

Being the bridge that can link the distance between you and your clients, social media is the path that you need to use to reach your market as quickly as possible.

Reaching Customers

Social media may be the only tool that can help you reach all age groups customers at once. These networks are not just for entertainment-seeking teenagers. More than 2.7 billion people are actively using social media platforms, so it's safe to say that whatever your target audience is, your potential customers are already spending some time on social media. Yes, a study found that 37% of all Americans over the age of 65 are fans of social media.

Social media is the perfect place to introduce your product/service to them, whether you want to meet young adults, housewives or retirees.

In fact, social media ads allow you to reach and retarget your customers, which can play a key role in your marketing strategy. For example, you can funnel ads on Facebook around your consumer's interests and target only the age, place, business, etc. of the market you're trying to reach.

Learning about Your Target Audience

Maybe the main reason social media marketing is so game-changing for businesses is because these networks actually allow you to have real interaction with your existing and potential customers. This creates an amazing opportunity to look inside the lives of your audience and learn first-hand about customer behaviors. You can easily find the answers to the questions that mostly concern every business by reading posts and tweets:

- What product/services are people interested in purchasing and why?
- That websites are mostly used by people?
- What are today's biggest interests and how can I improve my product/service?
- Which types of posts are most common to people?

Having the answers to these questions will help you understand your audience and allow you to write interesting posts and tweets that attract people. Through retweeting and linking, you will not only increase traffic and potentially benefit, but also discover what consumer deceptions are and how to improve your product/service to maximize conversion.

Getting Noticed Easily

Say you're organizing a gathering. There's a need for better promotion, right? What is the best way to do this than to have an active presence in social media? Social media platforms will help you spread the word that not only brings more guests, but can also give you some great advantages, such as finding donors who are eager to be involved.

Improving Your Brand's Image

Marketing your product/service on social media will help you grow as a company, increasing your brand's visibility, and make your identity identifiable and consistent.

The Best Customer Service Tool

Creating a great brand identity starts by making the customers happy and happy. Several surveys have shown that the majority of customers value certain companies that take the time to respond promptly to their inquiries. Yet it's not what it used to be to respond quickly to complaints. If a customer complaint is pending, the issue is required to be addressed immediately.

Social media lets you provide fast, supportive and responsive customer service and gives you the opportunity to meet your clients and support them before they can contact your call center. This little trick has just saved British Telecom's customer service bill by over 2 million pounds, so let that soak in for a second.

Building Up the Loyalty of Your Brand

This is, in truth, very self-explanatory, but not to mention it would be unfair. Through taking the time to actively engage with your customers and supplying them with valuable knowledge, assisting with questions, and keeping them happy without asking for anything in return, the value of your company is actually enhanced.

The best interaction on social media will bring value to consumers and convince them that you don't want to empty their pockets, but that you really care whether or not they're happy with your product / service.

CHAPTER 2

GETTING STARTED WITH SOCIAL MEDIA MARKETING

Posting family photos and check-in at the restaurant doesn't actually make you a master of social media. Even if you have an active account you use on a regular basis, there are many more things to consider when looking to use social networks as a powerful marketing tool. You need to stop seeing social media as a user, but rather as a business tool.

Did you know that between 9 am and 11 am Instagram has its highest traffic? Or that you can connect in six different ways on Twitter? Don't miss this chapter by assuming you're a social media specialist, so read on to see how you can scratch the surface to find the best way to continue selling on social media.

MAKING YOUR SOCIAL MEDIA MARKETING PLAN

Clear preparation for the future is indeed required in order to slay the competition and help your business succeed on social media. Your approach to social media marketing needs to take into account the real market image, your target audience's desires, and also your business wants and needs. If you don't know where to start and how to develop your perfect approach, these steps are most likely to help you create a decent plan:

1. **Check Your Social Media Presence**

If you're not just starting out, your company is likely to already be visible on some of the social media platforms. Take a good look at the networks and review where you are currently standing before you build a plan and go somewhere:
- What channels are you present on?
- Do you have optimized profiles?
- Is there a network that already offers you value?
- How does your profiles look like compared to the competition?

The next chapters will help you build killer profiles if you're not on social media. But before you do that, take a look at the profiles of the competitors to see what they offer at the moment.

2. Define Your Ideal Customer

Someone said the main marketing goal is to know exactly what your customers need in order for the product to sell on its own. Keep that in mind when you think of your ideal clients. If you want to stop selling to the wrong kind of crowd, you will need to be pretty specific.

You'll need to know exactly who your customer is before you actually start marketing. Here's a great example of how your customers should be defined: a 25-40-year-old stay-at-home mom who lives in the U.S., lives in a suburban house, uses Instagram primarily, and has something to do with crafts.

To identify the customer profile for which your product/service has been developed, answer the following questions:
- Age
- Position
- Type of employment and income
- Interests
- Stress points (which can be addressed by using your product/service)

- Most used social network.

3. Have a Social Media Marketing Mission Line

Some may think that this is crazy, but making a mission statement will help you stay focused at all times and keep your eyes on the ball. That's what drives all of your decisions, so make sure you get a good one. A mission statement will clarify what your primary objective is and what you expect to get out of social media marketing.

For example, a strong mission statement in social media marketing would say: "Use social media platforms to help people learn about healthy eating, provide organic, tasty free recipes, and advertise my new books." Of course, this is just one example. Your point of purpose can be anything you try to accomplish by marketing. Making sure all of your posts and tweets agree with that assertion is the main point. When you post blindly and without any driving goal, your marketing strategy is doomed to fail.

4. Decide on Your Metrics

To be effective in your social media marketing, you will need a good evaluation method. If you don't calculate your posts the right way, your content will not change, and you may even lose customers. That's why it is important to have a good measurement program.

How do you decide if your marketing strategies for social media are successful? What are the key metrics of success? What does it matter to you? Here are some metrics that can help you find the best way to market the products/service:

- Total Shares
- Conversion Rate
- Maximum The Company Mentions
- Time spent on your page

- Reach
- Sensitivity

5. Think About Investing in Social Media Management

If you're contemplating marketing on different platforms and being super-active on social media to reap the benefits, you're likely to get crunched over time. This ensures you may not be able to measure and monitor the progress of your marketing strategies for social media. To keep you up-to-date with the stuff your clients like most (as well as what they don't like) so you can change and add value, you need a social media management platform to increase productivity.

KILLER CONTENT IS THE KEY

Like any other marketing strategy, if there is no return on your social media marketing, you invested the wrong way. So your social media investment is the content that you publish.

Your customers expect value. If your posts aren't interesting then holding the viewer attention is quite impossible. After all, traffic to your website is powered by the content.

You will need to know precisely what types of content to post and why to make your social media marketing effective. And yes, there's more than one way to share.

User-Generated Content

The material that unpaid developers create is referred to as user-generated content. This makes sense if you think about it, as it is in our nature to try new products /services based on recommendations from other people to avoid making mistakes or deception. There is a high chance that we will respond positively to a picture shared by a friend than a photo shared by a brand. Not only will this type of content add credibility to your brand, it will also more humanely bind your business to your consumers.

GIFS

GIF is a popular type of image that supports images that are both static and animated. Thanks to its interesting visual features, this style of picture is particularly attractive to the younger population. Choosing to add GIFs to your website will give your viewers a reminder that you are tracking recent trends and that you are actually listening to them (whatever age group they belong to).

If you want your consumers to be captivated and visually stimulated, the right choice is to add GIFs.

INFOGRAPHICS

If you have to talk about a more complex subject, but you don't want to bore your customers with dense and dull reading, then graphics is the perfect choice. Properly designed graphics are not only capable of simplifying a complicated subject, but will also catch the attention of the consumer, even if they are not particularly interested in the subject. Infographics are an extremely valuable resource for promoting your social media, so be sure to integrate them whenever you get the opportunity.

Concept Visualization

Infographics are good and super powerful, but only if you don't try to tell a really long story. Instead, build them in a manner that will cover ample information and keep the interest of the client. Concept visualization is another powerful tool for simplifying complex topics.

Visualization of the idea is all those diagrams, maps, and images that are essentially self-explaining. Here, you can frame your tale in a simpler, enjoyable, and much more absorbable manner by demonstrating a single idea. In fact, they are more shareable than infographics, making them ideal for promoting the social media.

Live Steaming

Live streaming is a perfect way to attract visitors to your web, but that's not the only reason. You can also add additional information about your service or product while streaming and gaining more views and actually know that people are reading it. Live streaming is also perfect to connect with your clients through some Q&As and hear first-hand what they want.

CHAPTER 3

FACEBOOK

I'm not going to try to convince you why you need to start a Facebook account, because you really know how big Facebook is. Furthermore, when you say it like that, you need a Facebook page for your company, it sounds like a simple understatement. But I'll give you a taste of the latest statistics and explain why having a decent marketing strategy on Facebook can be of tremendous significance to your overall business.

While Facebook has basically been a big deal since the day it was invented, the marketing side now provides resources that we felt were not even conceivable 10 years ago. From selling services through your chat-bot to advertising your company in a 360-degree picture, Facebook marketing is a quality that must be followed by all companies.

The fact that Facebook has 2.27 billion active users, 1.49 billion of whom regularly use this site on a daily basis, is a pretty good reason why you should invest heavily in Facebook promoting the brand. If the average person spends 50 minutes a day on this site, you can only imagine how big this- network can be from a marketplace.

And while it's clear that Facebook is a crowded marketplace, it can be a terrible mistake for your company not to take advantage of the services it provides. Your competitor is already out there, selling their goods on this forum, being as big as it is, the chances are. It's just not something the company can afford to sit out. It may seem daunting, but if done correctly and with just the right amount of effort, you could also have impressive returns. Let this chapter guide you on a successful marketing journey.

Creating Your Facebook Page

First things first, you need to have a Facebook page up and running to advertise. By doing so, you're going to join 60 million businesses from around the world marketing their products on this platform. It sounds overwhelming, but this move is so crucial for that reason. It can really make a huge difference in the entire marketing process to create a killer website. You need to have a customized page first before you start posting quality content.

You already know how this works if you already have a personal account. Business pages are what people's profile pages are. By 'using' them as friends, users connect with people and join companies by 'liking' their accounts. Why am I mentioning this? If you want, by any chance, to open a profile instead of a page for your company, Facebook will permanently shut it down as it is against their rules.

You will see two different groups to choose from:

- Company or Product
- Community or Public Person

To start the process, click on 'Get Started' under 'Business or Brand'. The first thing you need to do is type the page's name. Think carefully about this because it's the label people are going to see. Changing the URL should be a choice for you, but still choose wisely.

You will pick the category under which your company falls after you have selected your name. Fill in the specifics like location, telephone number, etc. and press 'Start'.

You're going to be redirected to your new page as simple as that. Follow the tips from Facebook to customize your profile.

- **Profile Picture**

The major thing you need to take care of is to supply your business with a profile picture. Think of this image as the symbol of your business and make sure it's like a well-designed emblem that reflects your business well. The first message the company gives on Facebook is your profile picture, so make sure it is visible.

Uploading a 180x 180 pixel photo is preferred, but don't panic if you don't have a square frame. Facebook is going to suggest cropping, but the important thing is that all of the logo (if you upload a logo) suits in the cropped picture.

- **Cover Photo**

In comparison to your profile image, your cover photo, the horizontal image displayed at the top of your website, is what adds meaning to your account. This photo is usually used by businesses to promote special offers, discounts, etc.

To add your cover photo, simply click from your welcome menu on the 'Select a cover photo' button. The best resolution is 851x 315 pixels, but again, on Facebook, you can change your frame.

You can (and should!) regularly update your cover photo. To do this, simply click the 'Edit Cover' button found at the bottom corner on the right of your new cover.

- **Description**

You'll need a thoughtfully-written couple of sentences to describe your company to let people know what your business is all about. Facebook allows you to choose your words carefully with a maximum of 155 characters. Keep in mind that the search results will also include this summary, so make sure it is highly concise.

- **Username**

Your username is the name that shows in your Facebook URL, making it easier for customers to find you. You only have 50 characters for your username; make sure you use them for something special that other businesses don't already have.

- **Setting Up the Roles**

Now that the page's structure is over, it's time to set up the positions. The best thing about business pages is to keep them separate from your personal Facebook site. This means you're not the only person capable of editing the page. Certain users in your company can also hold the page without signing in through your personal account. It is up to you, however, to delegate the functions.

Admin: The page admin handles almost everything. This includes sending messages, responding to comments, posts being published and removed, ads, and even defining tasks. This person should be someone with the highest faith, so choose wisely.

Editor: Almost all the permissions as the admin, without the ability to assign roles.

Moderator: Comments can be addressed and removed by moderators, but do not have permission to post on the website. Nonetheless, they are allowed to advertise on Facebook.

Advertiser: The advertiser is only responsible for the promotional portion, as the name suggests.

Analyst: Only the reports can be monitored and the author reported what.

Live Blogger: The live blogger is someone who can go live (when live streaming) but is not allowed to post or respond to comments.

- **Call-to-Action**

Call to action is of great benefit. Facebook requires Pages to include a CTA button as of December 2014, which is a very convenient way for consumers to take action with your business. Tap on 'Add a button' above your cover and choose what the button will let customers to do: get in touch, download an app, buy a product, volunteer, book your services, etc., or add a link to your website, video, or other landing page.

- **Page Tabs**

It is advised that you add custom tabs to arrange the content that consumers will see on your website. This will allow your viewers the ability to see your videos, look for open jobs, go to your website, visit your Pinterest, etc.

There's a 'Manage Tabs' button in your left toolbar. To change your settings, click on it.

- **Verify**

It's as plain as that, consumers don't like unverified pages. This is not strictly mandatory, but it is encouraged if you want to add more value to your page and include a degree of authority. To enter your phone number, country, etc., go to 'Settings'—'General'—'Site Verification'. You will have to enter a verification code for Facebook.

- **Getting Your Fans**

It's time for you to get your first likes now that your Page is up and running. Having a 'like' from a client is them showing that they are interested in what you do and want to keep in touch with your products/services and promotions. Since the most successful business has millions of shares, the goal is to try to get as many of those "thumbs-ups" as you can.

Why Not Just Buy Likes?

It seems more convenient and easier, right? When you click "buy Facebook likes" on Google, all sales sets of likes for a fixed price will be forwarded to page. You may be tricked into thinking this will make your business look more successful and credible, but it's nothing but thin air for those likes. These so-called companies offering such kinds of likes use false or hacked identities and click farms. You won't get true feedback from an audience interested in your product/service. It's really doubtful that any of them will interact with your stuff, so the only thing you'll get is empty likes to buy them.

- **Promoting On Facebook**

You need to make sure to advertise your Page on Facebook the right way to get your views. Here are some tips to help you win likes:

- Be sure to make your username and page name straightforward
- Go through the section 'About' and customize everything. Include important keywords to help people find you faster on Google and other search engines
- Share your website with friends and get them to like it
- Lastly, be involved and connect with the fans you already have, as they bring more traffic to your page

- **Promoting Through Your Website**

Do not hesitate to spread the word and advertise your Facebook page there if you are fresh to Facebook but have a website that already has customers. You don't have to persuade them to do that; adding a page plugin with built-in Facebook iframe code to your website would enable your audience to like or even post your website without actually leaving your website.

- **Promoting Directly to Your Customers**

Another smart way to promote your Facebook page is to go directly to your customers. Do you have a store? For people to know you're online, design a fabulous Facebook sticker with your logo on it. Include the URL of your page in the top corner of the message when sending emails to your customers. On your slips, you can also include the Address. Do you want to be even more creative? Why not declare a promotion where you will be offering discounted prices on the spot in return for something like that.

POSTING LIKE A PRO
We've already talked about the importance of quality posts. Your content is the center of social media marketing and should be regularly posted as such. Think of the posts as your Page's food. The more you feed it, the greater it will rise. But just like the food you eat, the articles should be high quality and carefully selected as well.

To addition to the various types of content we talked about earlier, there are different ways to post on social media as well. Here are the various ways you can share your posts on Facebook with the world:

1. Facebook Images

Research have shown that Facebook image shares are 2.3 times more desirable and appealing to the viewer, which is why you should share these quality images with your clients.

Only click on 'Post a Photo or Video' under the blank post space to post an image on Facebook. Alternatively, to upload your image, you can start typing in the blank post and then click the camera button on the left.

The size of the images you will post is not that important (although it is recommended that 1200x 3600 pixels). The ratio is more important. With best results, make sure the ratio is 1.9:1.

2. Facebook Links

Sharing links to your products/services is the perfect way to feed your Profile. Whether you're writing blog posts about cooking or selling toys, your Facebook page requires updates to your new product/service to keep your fans up to date.

The same way you post a written post, you can post a link. Just paste the connection into the space of the blank article, and then write a short and entertaining summary. But wait, before you hit 'Post', avoid keeping the URLs to make the page look more professional. After posting the connection, remove the URL to make your post look new.

3. Facebook Video

Did you know that Facebook is going to be all video in the near future? That's no real surprise as the number of daily video views exceeds 8 billion. Facebook ads are watched every day for over 100 million hours. These are some important statistics that show us how appealing Facebook videos are for men.

The method of posting a video is the same as posting a photo. Tap on the 'Upload a Photo or Video' button and pick from your machine the requested image. The file format that is preferred is MP4 and MOV. Then add a line or two of text to your viewer explaining or presenting the video.

Keep in mind that Facebook immediately shows the first 5-10 seconds, which ensures that even if a person doesn't care about watching a video, they will see the beginning of your video as they scroll down their news feed. In order to appeal to people to hit the play button and watch the whole thing, try to make the start as appealing as possible.

4. Facebook Live

Facebook live is a feature that lets you to stream live content from your smartphone, unlike uploading pre-produced videos. To do this, open your phone's Facebook app and go to your profile. Click the button 'Publish' and then pick the alternative 'Live Stream'. Click 'Start' after allowing Facebook to access your camera and microphone.

You must enter certain privacy settings before you actually start watching. You can choose to stream to your friends, the entire audience, or just to yourself. Once you have decided to watch the film, you should write a line or two convincing others. The line goes hand in hand with your browsing, so make sure it's special and succinct.

Click 'Go live' and voila when you're ready to roll. You're on the board.

Click 'Stop' when streaming is finished. This will stop the streaming, but keep a record for later watching on your Page.

In interacting with the viewer this way, you show them that you are concerned not only with making a profit, but also with their feedback and happiness. Using Facebook Live to reach your customers can turn out to be a great marketing trick.

5. Facebook Instant Articles

As implied in his name, Facebook Instant Articles means reading on-the-spot articles without having to leave Facebook to move to another site. It's perfect because it saves time and it's pretty convenient.

Not all companies should take advantage of Instant Articles, but if you happen to be a writer, a lot of good stuff can be tossed in your way.

6. Virtual Reality

For Facebook, virtual reality is something you absolutely have to try if you have to tell a hypocritical story. And if you need to encourage some sort of special place or valuable experience, then you can't really afford to miss on this option. For a total pleasure, Facebook Virtual Reality allows you to share 360-degree images. This works best on mobile, and if recorded with a 360-degree camera it's the most appreciated, so think about investing in a good camera as part of your marketing strategy.

PIN YOUR POSTS

Pinning your posts involves choosing the order they appear on your blog. Facebook provides an opportunity to pin a post to the top of your website so that the first thing that attracts the customer's attention when they visit your page is your most important ads/promotions.

Do this by clicking on the arrow located in a post you previously shared in the top right corner. Then just press on' Pin to Page Bottom.' This is the article that will be shown at the top of your page before you pin another message.

OPTIMIZING FOR SEO

If you're curious if your Facebook page might have an effect on your ranking on Google, stop because it does. And I'm confident it will have a much greater impact than you can think. Here's the position that a good Facebook page will play in Search Engine Optimization (SEO):

- Will drive traffic to your website
- Could draw a highly relevant audience interested in what you're offering
- Build connections through your Facebook shares
- Using personalized keywords could increase your exposure

And if you're not sure how this process works, here's an illustration.

- You post your content on Facebook (add value)
- Your clients share your posts (building links)

- Friends of your friends see your content (boosting visibility)
- Friends of your friends and click to view the content (higher click-through rates)
- More people visit your website (higher traffic)
- More people engage with your company (low error rate)

This simple example simply gives you the opportunity to visit your website.

Keywords, Keywords, Keywords

You will optimize your Facebook posts with the use of appropriate keywords. You may have found that when looking for keywords, Google even lists the findings on social media. For example, if you type in an organic cotton clothing company, you will get results for the top organic cotton clothing companies websites and social media networks. That's because these firms have designed their blogs and profiles and included the organic, fiber, apparel, and business keywords, which is how you can find them online.

Optimizing your Facebook content will help people find out about you and easily learn about your business. But how are you going to do that? There are three different ways to add the right keywords and improve the profile of your business:

1. Optimize the URL

Make sure that the URL of your page includes the keywords most likely to be used by users to check for your online business.

2. Optimize your about section

You be unaware of this, but what you post on Facebook under 'About' can also help people find out about you online.

- Do analysis to see what are the most important keywords for your company
- Use 2 of the most appropriate keywords

- Creatively write down your definition, listing these keywords a few times
- Make sure that your business information is full. Business sites are often not classified at the top of Google Search due to lack of information. Type your exact location, phone number, website, and other important information that will help you find your clients.

Tip: Keep yourself safe! The appropriate keywords should be included in the definition, but at the same time sound moist and appealing. With the keywords you use, don't go overboard.

3. Optimize the posts you share

This may be the trickiest part because the effort to automate your posts should be constant and enforced on every post you think about posting.

Your post should also include important keywords, just like your 'About' section. For example, if you are promoting a new product, conduct research to see what the most important keywords are and include them in the message. If you're not a SEO wizard, you would seriously need to consider recruiting a professional.

THE RIGHT MARKETING STRATEGY

Let's discuss about some real business. Now that you know what your posts will look like and how to refine them for the best results, it's time for Facebook marketing's real challenge—finding the right approach, or in other words, what and when to write.

Let's move forward and think about some concrete tactics, considering you really know who the target is.

If you don't know your audience's persona, you can use an Audience Insights tool. This incredible method will allow you to get your audience's behavioral and demographic data to determine what kind of content people are actually searching for.

Social Media Content Calendar
If you don't use a social media management tool, all Facebook posts must have a content calendar. It doesn't have to be fancy. Your content calendar can be a basic spreadsheet where you will write and assign your posts for different times in advance. Here are some ideas for a great social media content calendar:
- Have sections for each of your sites (this calendar is not only for Facebook but also for the other social media networks)
- Have a day-to-day post schedule split into time slots
- Set some columns with specific details such as the hashtag name, photos you want to share with, the number of letters, a brief message to send.
- Give space for a monthly view of your posts to keep track of large campaigns

Scheduling Your Posts
Although keeping a social media calendar can be a real life saver when it comes to social media marketing, if you don't regularly plan your posts on Facebook, you will never be able to take a break. If you plan to market on this platform successfully, you will need to be super-active and regularly post it. If you're crunched for time and not always open, that can be tricky. Fortunately, Facebook gives you a great option to prepare your posts in advance.
The method is quite clear. Rather than clicking 'Publish' and posting the post after it was published, click on the arrow next to 'Publish' and instead pick 'Schedule'. Input the time and date, and all of you are sorted.

You can always reschedule or postpone if you have a change of heart, don't stress. Just click the 'Publishing Tools' at the top of your page and choose Rescheduling, Canceling Calendar, Backdate, or Deleting.

When to Post and How Often?

It's cool to plan your posts, but if you don't actually know when the time is right for publishing, it might not be that helpful. So, when is it the right time to post on Facebook's? And how often will the posts be shared?

If you came here in search of a clear answer to your business, let me break it to you—there's no one. It depends on many factors when and how often to post on Facebook: if your target is in the same time zone, your place, your main goal, what your business is about, etc. There are some tricks to get your sleeve up, though.

Follow these rules
WHEN TO POST:

- The rule of a thumb is that your posts will be seen by more people if you aim between 1 p.m. and 5 p.m. on weekdays, and on the weekends between 12 and 1 p.m.
- Saturday and Sunday are the perfect days for posting on Facebook, followed by Friday and Thursday, so save the most important posts for those days.
- On Fridays, people are happy, so save this day's positive and optimistic stories.
- Research has shown that posting on Facebook at 3 p.m. will give you more likes, while the 1 p.m. posts will give you more shares, so keep this in mind when posting.

HOW OFTEN TO POST:

The law of a thumb says you should post between 1 and 2 posts per day when it comes to how often the posts should be. You would think posting will often mean further interaction, but in reality it's quite the reverse. Research has shown that repeated posts lead to a reduction in the audience.

Another rule of thumb is that sharing more than 1-2 times a day can only help successful businesses with more than 10,000 followers. Posting businesses with less than 10,000 likes more than 2 times a day can carry 60% less views, statistics show.

It's important to remember that content trumps often over size, so don't be concerned with how often the posts should be. Alternatively, make sure the material is well developed, built and appropriate for the right audience.

Facebook Bots

A bot is an AI program that people interact with to ask for some information or to complete a specific task automatically. Facebook bots have taken over the Messenger absolutely and are particularly important for businesses.

Just as users use Messenger to chat with friends, they can also use this app to connect with bots and ask for alerts, change the shipping address, ask for hours of work, order products, etc. Through getting rid of repetitive clicking through the company's page to find what they're looking for, interacting with bots makes consumers shopping experience much more comfortable. Half of the people are actually interested in shopping from an artificial bot, so be sure to add a chatbot to your Facebook page.

There are plenty of tools to help you build a chatbot. One of the most popular is Chatfuel.

Generating Leads

Leads are potential clients. These are the people who have shown interest in your product or service but have not yet paid consumers. For example, if someone has subscribed to a free trial, downloaded your eBook's free portion, or signed up for a promotional product, that user is a member.

To convert your leads into clients, you need a good strategy on how to create leads and share information that they will find attractive:

- Uploading special offers landing pages
- Scheduling Facebook meetings for the next webinar
- Making and uploading videos to highlight special lead generating opportunities

- Posting Facebook Lives to inform the followers about upcoming events
- Sharing blog posts that have already proved to generate leads

Of course, be careful not to overdo it. Not all of the material should be the lead generation. Combine things and find the right balance that works best for your company.

You can use Facebook Lead Advertising to receive lead data from Facebook. This is a great feature that will provide the followers with links to your special offers, without leaving the Facebook app.

Tracking Your Results

Now that you know some tricks that can give you more views, hearts, and shares, it's time to learn how to search to see if your marketing efforts are actually paying off. Your marketing strategy won't have a proper plan to document results that will involve a lot of assumptions and expectations that can lead to under-realization.

Facebook has created a tool called Facebook Insights for this purpose that can help you analyze, track and measure your success.

Tap the 'Insights' tab at the top of your page to join this device. Once you do that, you will be led to your Page's 'Profile', which is the last week's operation of your Page. You can look at this, but you need to go through the tabs on the left if you want to find out some more specific details.

- **Like**. The segment Like will show you how many likes for each day you have got so far. You're going to see a graph showing your results. There you will see the graph of Net Likes, which is what most people should be interested in, and that is the number of likes minus the number of unlikes.

- **Reach**. Check the Reach tab if you want to see how people are engaging with your content. There you will find a graph of post engagement divided into organic traffic (naturally occurring traffic) and paid traffic (the traffic you pay for and directly target through advertising to specific consumers).

- **Page views**. This will inform you not only how many times your website has been viewed, but also how many visitors have entered your page. You can also read about what people usually do on your Site upon landing here.

- **Posts**. This is probably the most useful option offered by this app, as it allows you to understand when your followers are online, which can be a great help during your scheduling posts process. Posts show reviews, feedback, updates, post hides, complaints or spams from your followers, engagement levels, etc. If you want a quick check of your posts progress without having to go through Page Insights, just click on the 'People Reached' button right above the 'Recommend' button and you can automatically go through the posting info.

ADVERTISING ON FACEBOOK

You need to follow a series of three different elements to promote your products or services on Facebook:
- Campaign
- Ad Sets
- Ads

This section will help you learn everything about Facebook ads and how to optimize the results with the least budget and effort.

1. Facebook Ad Campaign

Once you start the ad creation process, Facebook will ask you to pick your favorite editor, which will be either Ad Manager or Power Editor. Both of them have ups and downs based on what you're looking for. The Ad Manager is most popular as it is more flexible, but if you're a big company looking for greater precision and leverage over multiple campaigns, then the Power Editor might be a better fit.

Let's say you're happy with Ad Manager for this reason. There's a drop-down menu in the right upper corner of your screen. Tap on it, and then choose 'Form Ads'.

You'll be asked to pick a target for your initiative. In all, you can find 11 targets, grouped into 3 groups. Choose the most fitting one for you. The formal campaign start-up cycle has been finished.

2. The Ad-Sets

Once the initial process is over, the steps to identify the target, set the budget, and plan and refine the ad collection should be followed.

• Audience

If you've already used this tool, Facebook already knows your audience. If not, insert your target audience's defined details such as gender, age, location, and language. You might add more filters after that, for example, by targeting only the people who enjoyed a single post or something like that.

Make sure it's the picked' Automatic Placements' under' Placements.'

• Budget

There are two typed budgets to choose from:

Daily Budget –choose this alternative if your goal is to advertise constantly. Enter the number you're comfortable spending for this particular ad on a daily basis.

Lifetime Budget–If you have a defined amount of time you want to run the ad for, choose this choice. There, for that time, the budget will be spread evenly.

- **Schedule**

Now it is time for your ad collection to be prepared. You can either immediately start the promotional cycle or set a start and end date for your commercial.

- **Optimization**

Click the button 'View Advanced Options' and pick the configuration you want. Here, you choose the option to optimize your advertisement to allow Facebook to show people the ad that will pay the most attention.

Click ' Start ' if you're ready.

CREATING THE AD

Now it's time to select the size, text, internet, and links to create your Facebook ad:

- First, choose the style choices you want. Facebook will give you options (carousel, single picture, slideshow, single photo, etc.) so you can choose the one that looks most interesting to you.
- Now that the look of your ad has been picked, upload the materials and write a captivating ad headline. Facebook will provide template recommendations based on the format chosen.
- Update, polish, demo, finish the design.

TIPS FOR SUCCESSFUL ADVERTISING

Here are some tips that can improve the promotional cycle and, in effect, raise your organic ad-paid traffic:

- **Focus on video**

Video ads produces much more views than those based on images. How-to videos, customer-testimonial videos, and tasteful videos of product presentation will help you create a lot of business.

- **Go for a Lookalike audience**

A lookalike audience is a very close group of people. This is a great trick for advertisements, as you can literally create a list of clients (or even leads) and post it to Facebook to build your lookalike audience. Go to your Ad Manager to import this, open 'Audiences' and pick the alternative 'Lookalike Audience'.

- **When retargeting be specific**

As you retarget your crowd, do not just retarget them as a group, but try to get as specific as possible. For example, choose only those customers who have viewed a particular part of your website or purchased a particular type of product based on what you are selling.

- **Download Facebook Pixel**

Facebook Pixel, the main Facebook advertising tool, is a simple program that you put on your website that collects data and lets you not only keep track of your purchases, but also build followers, configure your ads and even point out.
To build your Facebook picture, go to your Facebook Events Administrator and pick 'Pixels'. Then click 'Create a Pixel', type your pixel name, and then select 'Save'. You will need to load some software on your website to connect the Pixel to your website, but this mostly depends on the application you use.
This can be done easily if you use an e-commerce website, because Facebook can provide you with a support article explaining the entire process.

If you are collaborating with a client, the Developer's Email Instructions option can be chosen.

You can also manually download the Code Yourself, in which case you are going to copy and paste the code into your website's header file.

- **Try the Callout Method**

It may seem cliché, but to call people's attention seems to be a trick as old as time. But who knows for as long as it works? In order to tell your target, try to start the ad with a few questions.

For example, if you're marketing your weight loss book, you might want to start as follows: "Tired of eating boring greens for the sake of your flat belly? Would you like to have both a big tummy and a slim figure? I have the perfect idea for you..." and add a few words to describe your email.

This strategy has the advantage of being able to use it as an additional tool for entering customers. Such people whose diets are ineffective, who are always hungry and discouraged, and who are looking for a better way to lose weight, for example, are the target audience. Who are you offering precisely?

- **Stick to the 20%-or-Less Text Rule**

With more than 20 percent of the text, it was Facebook's practice to immediately reject picture advertising. They may no longer be so stringent and sometimes even need such ads, but it is a fact that people reply better to the picture. Try to minimize the text by choosing the right words intentionally and making the logo the focus of the commercial.

The Boost Post

Although it is not necessarily an advertising strategy, another great way to boost the post is the 'Boost Post' tool that Facebook provides. When is this to be used? Unless you're a super-successful company with millions of fans, from time to time you're going to have to hit the 'Boost Code'. It's time to use additional tools to improve your organic scope when your post doesn't pull enough traffic to your website. In addition to helping you increasing your organic traffic, the' boost message ' button will also give you the opportunity to reach a wider audience.

For example, it will cost you some money to boost your post and share it on Facebook. Yet you can't be more wrong if you think it's going to break the bank. Just like Facebook ads, you'll be able to set your own schedule, so you'll end up paying the price you're happy with. The minimum amount is $1 per week, so note that the more money you spend, the better will be the target audience.

1. Choose Your Post

Whether it's the one you're currently creating or an earlier post, choose the one you'd like to show to your public and press the 'Boost Post' button in the bottom right corner of your page.

2. Target Your Audience

Facebook will give you the option to select options to attract the right audience for you after selecting the post you want to raise. Through choosing the choice 'Create New Audience' and specifying it as you want, you can easily create a new audience through setting the age range, venue, different preferences and other important factors.

3. Set Your Budget

You should have a pretty realistic understanding of how much you need to invest on your boosted post after identifying your target. Once, you should spend at least $1, but you know that higher budgets are equal to greater scope.

4. Set the Duration

Then you need to choose the number of days that you want to improve your message. The default is set for 1, 7 and 14 days, but a specified date can also be entered.

5. Preview the Boosted Post

Now is the time to take a look at your ad to make sure it looks decent (links work, it's error-free, etc.) because this is your last chance to correct any mistakes before your post actually goes live.

6. Choose Your Payment Option

Choose the form to pay for your raise posts that you want to use. Click 'Continue' to fill in the details.

7. Boost

You're able to improve at last. To check the status of the enhanced email, under 'Ads Director' you should search the 'Delivery' tab.

CHAPTER 4

YOUTUBE

I'm sure everybody who's ever been using the Internet knows how huge YouTube is. Actually, I'm pretty sure we've all wasted a whole lazy day watching funny YouTube videos at some point, too. But what everyone doesn't know is that this platform has also become a crucial tool for successful marketers from around the world, in addition to its ability to entertain.

YouTube is the 2nd largest search engine with over 1.8 billion monthly users (who are actually logged in), over 1 billion hours of watched videos per day, and over 400 hours of video uploaded every minute.

Whatever category they may fall into, chances are, there is already a huge chunk of your target audience on YouTube. YouTube content marketing is a smart move that will help your brand grow by giving your customers more value.

CREATING YOUR BUSINESS PROFILE

Firstly, we need to be certain that you have an active Google account before we hop right to set up your YouTube account and build your profile. YouTube is owned by Google, as you may remember, and you can sign in to YouTube by owning a Gmail account.

But wait before opening YouTube and start the process of creating a profile. It may not be such a good idea to connect your YouTube profile to your existing email, particularly if we're talking about your business Gmail account. It is not recommended to share your access to your YouTube profile with anyone in your company who has access to your business email. Using a new Gmail account is wise for this purpose:

- Go to www.google.com and click the 'Sign Up' button in the upper right corner.
- Go to 'Build'—'Build Account'.
- By inserting your name, email addresses, address, birthday, etc., fill in the information and press 'Next step.
- If a code number is sent, verify your account by entering your phone number. Click 'Next' to type in the file. Your new account for Gmail is now up and running.

Now that you've got a Gmail account, it's time to set up and build your brand's own YouTube account.

Just visit www.youtube.com to get going. You're actually only logging in with YouTube if you're signed in with your Gmail. If not, in the upper right corner, click the 'Sign In' button and enter your Gmail and password. Tap on the Gmail account button in the upper right corner once you're in, and pick 'My Channel'. You will have the option to automatically build your site, but choose 'Use a Business or Other Title' from the bottom of the page for your intent. Type in your brand's name now and then press 'Edit'. Keep in mind that from the settings menu, this can be changed later.

Channel Icon and Channel Art

Now that you've created your channel, it's time to customize it. Only click the 'Edit Template' button and let's go. The first thing you need to do is build an icon and art site. YouTube's channel icon and channel art are what Facebook's profile image and cover image are—they're the first thing your visitors see and so leave the first impression.

To add your channel icon, click on the default red button. Choose an image from your machine, but bear in mind that your Grail and Google+ accounts will also use this photo. It is advised to use 800x 800 pixels.

First, press the 'Add channel art' button in your channel center and upload your favorite image. Recommended pixel here is 2560x 1440.

Describing Your Brand

It's time to add some info about your business after uploading your pictures and configure the "About" page. Write a concise summary that will quickly describe your business and also let people know about the kind of videos that will be posted to your website. Be sure to include links to your website and other social media platforms as well as your email address for your business.

A great option YouTube offers is the fact that for unsubscribed and subscribed users you can customize your channel differently. The best way to use this choice is to add a channel trailer to hit the 'subscribe' button, which will lure visitors.

The channel trailer is your channel's video description and should be short (not longer than 90 seconds; the best is 45 seconds) and attractive. The main purpose should be to accept and inspire tourists to subscribe.

It's time to upload it once you've made your channel trailer:

- Make sure the channel configuration is on. Upon clicking on the settings icon next to 'subscribe you can test this. Select the 'Customize your channel layout' and press 'Save' afterwards.
- To import your trailer, press the arrow button at the top right corner. Choose the correct file from your computer and, once it is saved, click on 'To New Users'.
- Select 'Network Preview', pick the file that you imported, and click 'Save'.

Once you've got your first 100 subscribers, your channel is over 30 days old, and you've uploaded a channel icon and art, your YouTube profile will be eligible for a unique, customized URL that will give you a more professional look.

Appointing the Roles

You will decide how many members of your staff will have access to the YouTube channel of your business and what their tasks will be before you actually start uploading videos to launch your YouTube marketing strategy.

When you give them access to the Google account, there are three different roles to choose from:

Owner–they will have full power so they will add/remove employees, answer/remove comments or complaints, edit content, etc.

Manager–Managers can have all the access to editing as the owner without adding or removing other managers.

Communications manager–The communications manager, as the name suggests, is primarily responsible for interacting with the public. They will respond to comments and reviews and do other editing options, but they are unable to upload new content, view analytics, or use the video manager.

Go to'overview'—Add or remove administrators' and add your YouTube account to handle people.

OPTIMIZING FOR SEO

So, you built your business channel for YouTube successfully. Congratulations! But successful marketing has so much more to do than simply creating and uploading engaging videos. People will have to search your videos first before they can watch it. Yet how can they do that if you haven't structured the 'metadata' of your videos?

Your video metadata is what gives people information about the video, such as its title, genre, image, annotations, background, subtitles, etc., and providing the right kind of metadata can make it easy for your viewer to find your video on YouTube or Google Search.

- **Title**

The first thing people notice about a video while browsing through the results on YouTube is its title and thumbnail. The title is what attracts the attention of the audience and should therefore be well-thought-out. In order to understand what people are looking for, conduct a research. Then include in the title the relevant keywords and important information, but be cautious not to go overboard. If your title has more than 60 characters, the video result pages on YouTube will show a cut-off, and people may not even read the whole thing. Keep it simple, straightforward, and strong.

- **Description**

Like your theme, the video description should also include important keywords that help potential viewers quickly find your video. But as important as the definition is, it's important to remember that most people don't really bother reading it. That is, unless they're involved. Your job is to impress them. YouTube typically only shows the description's first 2-3 lines. When viewers want to read the rest of it, the remaining material must be pressed on the 'show more' button. Make sure that the beginning of the summary is polished and re-polished as much as it takes to make it interesting so that the readers want to read the whole material.

If your explanation includes CTAs or some relevant connections that you want to share with your readers, make sure that they are included in the summary at the top so users can see them even without pressing 'display more'.

Another point is to always include a transcript of your video when writing the summary. Why? Because the keywords complete the video itself. You will significantly improve your SEO by writing a short transcript with these keywords and finally the ranking of your company.

- **Tags**

Tags are perfect because they can connect the videos of your brand with other popular YouTube videos and that only extends your scope and increase your exposure. To this end, make sure the keywords are labeled. First of all, identifying the most important keywords is a crucial part of the SEO optimization of your brand, so make sure you pick your words wisely.

- **Category**

After the video is uploaded, the category in which it will be shown on YouTube must be chosen. Under 'Advanced settings', you can select the video category. You can choose from Film & Animation, Travel & Events, Entertainment, Music, Pets & Animals, Educations, Nonprofits & Activism, People & Blogs, Sports, Cars & Vehicles, How-to & Style, Science & Technology, News & Politics, and Comedy.

It is very important to choose your category carefully, as the categories are what group your videos on YouTube along with the relevant ones. For example, you may not reach your target audience if you sell dog shampoo and list your video in People & Blogs instead of Pets & Animals.

- **Thumbnail**

As mentioned above, your video's thumbnail is extremely important as it is the first thing people see on YouTube since finding your video along with the description. The thumbnails have a important impact on the number of views and should be carefully selected. Although after uploading, YouTube will offer a few auto-generated thumbnails option, it is highly recommended that you skip this option and instead include a custom thumbnail. Choose a picture that allows people to click and is a good light for your video. YouTube says 90 percent of YouTube's most popular videos actually have custom thumbnails, but with this one you can't be wrong.

- **SRT Files**

Closed captions and subtitles are extremely useful to audiences, but that is not the only reason why they should be included in the video. Even, SRT files are a great way to highlight the keywords. SRT files are a powerful SEO optimization resource that you should definitely take advantage of, whether you choose to add a timed subtitles file or a transcript of your text.

Go to 'video manager'—'Videos' for inserting SRT videos. Choose the video you want to connect the SRT files to and choose the drop-down arrow on the right side. Click 'Subtitles/CC' and click the correct subtitles.

- **End Screens and Cards**

YouTube provides a convenient option to add end screens and cards that can help encourage the fans to visit your website, check out other posts, and even answer poll questions.

Cards are the little reminders that usually appear in your video's top right corner. Your card may include a poll, a link, another video, or you may use it to support another YouTube channel. At the same time, you should add up to 5 cards, but be vigilant because too many inquiries tend to put off viewers. When you really have to add a few cards, make sure that they are well spread out so that the audience can take several acts without feeling overwhelmed.

Go to 'Video Manager'—'Cards'—'Add Card' to add a card and choose whether to create a link, camera or playlist, screen, or poll card. Just drag the card to where you want it to appear on the video after it has been created.

End Screens are the last seconds of the video that allow people to take further action such as subscribing to the page, visiting a Facebook Including end screens and cards is a valuable option offered by YouTube that can help encourage the audience to access your website, review your other posts, and even answer poll questions.

End Screens are the last seconds of the video that allow viewers to take additional action, such as subscribing to the website, visiting a Facebook page, pressing the like button, trying out another video, etc. You should add an additional 5-20 seconds to your videos and invite your viewers to join your brand.

Tap on the drop-down arrow and pick 'End Screens and Notes' to connect an end screen to'video manager'. There, you can choose which things to include the end screen, just keep in mind that you need to promote another YouTube video or playlist, because even if you just wanted to encourage users to visit your website, you'd also need to persuade people to watch some other company video there.

- **Playlists**

You may think it's not worth your time to build playlists, but this tool is a real gem for YouTube advertisers. What's the reason? Because it increases your visibility. You can blend videos not only from your sites, but also from other YouTube channels by building your playlists. And the best part is that the search results list these playlists perhaps display them individually. For example, if you make a collection of your videos and include some popular ones with similar content, you're going to help other people who may not have heard of your brand before, find out.

Click the'+' button below your video to create a playlist, select 'Create new playlist', pick your playlist name, and click 'Create'. Simply use the same button to add more videos, but instead of clicking on 'Create new playlist', select the existing one to display your videos.

MAKING THE VIDEOS

Now that your YouTube channel is all set up and you know what to do to refine it for SEO, the next move is to learn how to make great videos that people are actually going to watch. After all, high-quality videos are the most important part of YouTube marketing. If your videos are not properly made, targeting the right audience, your high-class approach won't have much meaning.

So let's continue to fill your channel with fantastic content;

Type of YouTube Videos

Before you say "Action" and start filming, you must first decide what your video will be like. There are eight types of videos that are typically created by YouTube marketers:

1. Customer Testimonials

Testimonials from consumers are something any popular business can record and post to their YouTube channel at some point. These are short interview-like videos in which satisfied consumers are shot in order to express their pleasure with the product/service, share their positive experience with others, and promote the company to anyone who finds their products or services.

2. Explainer Videos

Explainer videos are also referred to as tutorial videos or how-to videos and, as the name suggests, their main purpose is to illustrate how to use a certain product or service to viewers. These are also a very detailed and thoughtful way to explain customer support issues that are more nuanced.

3. On-Demand Demonstration Videos

Demonstration videos are usually short videos that are filmed in order to demonstrate quickly the use of a certain product or service and to show its advantages to potential customers.

4. Case Studies and Project Reviews

Whether it's the case studies of a successful campaign or the 5-star ratings of a particular product, these videos seek to recapture the positive results and share them with the world and turn potential customers into shoppers.

5. Thought Leader Interviews

These videos are quality interviews with niche experts with the sole purpose of enhancing your brand's credibility.

6. Video Blogs

Video blogs or vlogs are often posted (on a daily or weekly basis) documenting certain events. YouTube marketers are popular with video blogs as they are a great way to get people to visit your website. Through summarizing a specific blog post and uploading the video to your YouTube channel, you also provide multiple options for your consumers to digest your content.

7. YouTube Live

YouTube Live is a feature that enables you to live broadcast to your subscribers. This amazing feature is extremely valuable for your marketing strategy as it enables you to connect live with your audience and allows them to engage in real-time discussions.

8. Event Videos

Event videos are those videos that show the knowledge of a meeting, auction, or other event, and are a great way to share with your online viewers the positive reaction of the current audience.

THE SCRIPT OF YOUR VIDEOS

Now that you have selected your video form, it's time for your script to be carefully crafted. There are a few steps you need to take care of before you start filming to ensure that the video gives value.

- **The Goal**

You must first determine what that idea should accomplish before you turn your idea into reality. What's your video's goal? By adding it to your page, what are you trying to achieve? Do you want the number of subscribers to increase? Boost knowledge of your brand? More traffic to your page?

You want all these things, of course, but a particular objective is the key to making a good video to be viewed. Make each video with a single aim in mind. This will help you stay fixated and at one point avoid dealing with different things, which is the best marketing strategy.

- **Create the Story**

Now that's the creative part. It's time to wake up your mind after deciding your target and create a good narrative for your film. This should serve as a guide and description for the shooting process. A good video storyboard should include:
- A frame for each scene
- Short description for each scene
- Lines for each scene
- Camera instructions and shooting details (for example, wide shots, close shots, etc.).

- **The Extra Elements**

When you plan to include additional visual features such as slides or graphics in your images, then you should prepare for them in advance. Make sure that the extra content is placed and added to your storyboard without any errors.

- **The Length of the Video**

How long is your video going to be? This is an important factor in the process of video making so make sure that this is determined as soon as possible. Videos under 2 minutes have the highest level of audience engagement on YouTube, so bear that in mind when determining how long the key message will take.

- **The Filming Location**

You may need one, two or more filming locations depending on the type and definition of your recording. It can be tricky to find the right shooting spot, so you may want to get your friends and family involved to help you out with this one. Whatever you choose, note that you may need a shooting permit for some places, so take care of this one in advance to avoid being sued.
Visit every venue before filming to decide how to change the scenery, take care of the setting, take care of the ambient sounds, etc.

SHOOTING A HIGH-QUALITY VIDEO
Unless you're a very successful business and can afford to pay an expensive shooting crew to take care of the video making process for you, you're going to need some technical tips to help you make high quality videos that can be viewed. Whether you're using your mobile or a semi-professional video camera, the following tips will help you add professional content to your channel:

- **A Tripod Is a Must**

The first impression is often the most critical, especially when attempting to represent the brand and sell products/services. If a faulty camera starts your film, nobody will watch it, ever. People are looking to hear the story behind it when they click on the video, not to be disturbed by the unprofessional shooting. If your shot is shaky, buy a decent tripod for a professional look that will hold your camera steady.

- **Go for Different Angles**

Visually dull is a scene that is filmed from just one perspective. Shoot each scene from a few different angles to spice things up so you can edit it later and make an appealing, expensive-like video.

- **More is More**

Make a habit of shooting more than you ever like. This will only give you additional content to choose from during the process of editing and will only take a little more money. After all, cutting what you don't need is always fast. Going back and re-filming is not just a challenge, but difficult at times.

- **Choose the Manual Mode**

I read somewhere that actual photographers only use manual mode because they can tell the camera what they want and there are no awkward surprises like automation. If this option is available to your computer, go to a full manual mode to get the most out of shooting. So you can easily adjust the focus and shoot a video that is beautifully pleasing.

- **Invest in Your Microphone**

If your video involves voice, then it's not a choice to invest in a high quality microphone—it's a must. From the end of a tunnel you don't want to look like you're referring to your audience. Even if you use your mobile for the video making process, you can buy a microphone that can be inserted into your system to improve your video's sound even further.

EDITING YOUR VIDEO
It's time to edit the video material after shooting to create a convincing high quality video that can be posted to your YouTube channel.

- **Editing Tools**

Your OS already has some editing software that provides basic editing tools including color correction, clip clipping, or title adding. If you want a more professional-looking video, though, it is highly recommended to spend some money on more advanced software such as Adobe Premier CC or Final Cut Pro X. YouTube also offers online editing software for this purpose if you want to keep things pretty low-budget.

- **Thumbnails**

Image thumbnails, as discussed earlier, are extremely important. The video preview is what potential viewers will see on your YouTube channel, as well as their recommended column on their right showing similar videos of their video search results. YouTube's most popular advertisers are posting their own custom thumbnails, so get creative and make yourself one.

- **Watermarks**

Would you like to invite your audience to press the button 'subscribe?' Then it's a perfect choice to add a watermark. Watermarks are custom-made 'subscribe' buttons put on your videos to catch the viewer's attention and allow them to select and subscribe to your channel while watching your video.
Go to 'Creator Studio'—'Channel'—'Branding' if you want to add a watermark. Click' Add a watermark' and follow the instructions for uploading.

- **Sound Effects**

Probably the most important aspect making the difference between a professional-shot video and an inexperienced one on a low budget is high-quality sound effects. But to have movie-like songs, you don't have to have a huge budget. There are now many ways to add a sound of consistency to your videos without exhausting your budget.

YouTube offers a range of high-quality sound effects to choose from for your posts. But if you're not so excited about that decision, it may be your best solution to find royalty-free music online. You can still stream royalty-free sounds for free, but if you want to add a more professional feel to your videos, think about saving some money and buying the right music for a flat price for your video. Royalty-free means that you are free to use the music file any way you see fit when you pay for the album, even if the video skyrockets on YouTube, without having to make any additional payments.

MARKETING THE VIDEOS

Now that your video is shot, perfectly edited and posted to your YouTube channel effectively, the next step is to find the best marketing plan and get people to actually select and view your video.

If you haven't noticed it, we've already covered a lot of YouTube marketing strategies that will help people discover and watch your videos like: using relevant keywords, using tags, having a rich and compelling description, having the perfect thumbnail image, including descriptive transcripts, using cards and end screens, and combining your videos with popular ones in playlists. Let's call them all tricks, all of these will help boost organic traffic, get more views, and improve your ranking. But if you've just jumped on the YouTube marketing ride, sticking out and meeting your targets might be quite challenging. YouTube marketing's initial (and most important!) strategy is to know how to spread the word.

The first thing you need to do is spread the word and let your fans know you've got a YouTube channel where they can check out your content.

- **Social Media**

Do you have an account on Facebook or Instagram? The best way to let your followers know about your channel and videos and get them involved is to post your content on other social media platforms. Fortunately, it couldn't be easier to share YouTube videos. To share a video, simply click the 'Post' button below the video and pick the content marketing platform. Another option is to copy the video URL while the video is running from the address bar and then paste the link on your social media page.

Yet keep in mind that it's not a good marketing tactic to post the video alone. You don't post with your friends a stupid cat video; you need people to watch and get interested. Always think about why you first made the video while talking about sharing a video. Was it a tutorial to simplify the usage and answer questions from the customer? If so, the best way to answer these questions is to share your video. Was that part of a trend or campaign? If that was the reason, then don't forget to make sure your video is part of a conversation with the important #hashtags. Or if you just want to spread awareness around your business, it can also be very helpful to include the link to the video in your 'About' section.

- **Website**

The perfect place to advertise your YouTube channel and videos is your website or blog. Do not hesitate to include 'Support' buttons on your social media platforms if you have a website that is up and running. That also includes Twitch. This will allow visitors to your site to locate your channel quickly and to keep up-to-date with your video posts by pressing the' Subscribe' button.

A great strategy is also to create a video that will be shared as an introduction to some analysis, case study, or just blog post. It works both ways because not only can it help you sell your content and earn more views on YouTube, it can also boost direct traffic to your website and other channels.

To upload one of your YouTube videos on your website, find underneath the video the embed code, copy it, and paste it where you want it to be displayed.

- **Email**

The worst mistake advertisers can make is to think about finding a new audience and losing the ones they already have. It's time to share the news with your existing users/customers when your YouTube channel is filled with some videos. And what better way to do this than with a list of emails? Give a helpful information and video email newsletter and invite your clients to connect with your business. You don't like to send links of your videos to your customers? How about welcoming them to check out a certain website post that has already embedded your YouTube video?

- **Collaboration**

Sometimes the solution is in the hands of somebody else. If your brand has a YouTube channel in partnership with another organization, invite them to work together. For both companies, this will not only be fun and exciting, but it's the best way to join together and grow the market. You will end up getting a lot of their viewers and vice versa by making a video or even a playlist together. However, the main thing to keep in mind is that your priorities are identical and cooperation with the other company is consistent with your approach.

- **Q&A Websites**

Have you ever been to a Q&A website? They are the perfect place to get experts and people with experience in the field of your interest to find a solution to your questions. The most popular site at the moment is www.quora.com. Allow the most of it. Monitor the types of questions people ask and provide your video content with solutions. Who knows about it? This may turn out to be the best strategy for marketing out there.

- **Engage, Engage, Engage!**

Lastly, it can be quite simple to find a solution. Engage the current customers to expand their happiness and positive experience. Answer your questions, respond to your comments in a timely manner, ask for honest their feedback and don't forget to thank them for their support. This is the job that is hardest but easy to overlook. Make sure that you are there for the customers are there so that they can be there for you.

GETTING A HANDLE ON YOUTUBE ANALYTICS

You cannot really be effective in spending your time and effort in making and posting quality and supportive videos to your YouTube channel until you calculate what you have accomplished. Keeping track of your success will help you identify what you're doing well, what works best, and what needs to be improved to maximize success and increase your ranking on YouTube.

Every YouTube channel has its YouTube Analytics which provides information on the success of the channel over a certain period of time. Knowing just what these numbers and figures mean will help you get a clear picture of whether or not viewers are finding your videos appealing. Here's a short guide on how to measure success with Analytics:

Your Goal

You can't expect to calculate your performance if you don't have a specific goal in mind, because you don't have a benchmark for your metrics. Knowing why you are sharing your video (remember, one goal per video?) will help you visualize where you see your video and where it actually stands. It helps you to understand which places need to be changed and whether you should consider investing in paid ads to bring more traffic to your website.

Now that you've remembered what you're expecting to do with your videos, it's time to check whether or not they've been delivered. Enable your YouTube Analytics is the first thing you need to do. Just go to www.youtube.com/analytics (log in for sure). Upon entering, you should see a 28-day performance overview of your videos. The timeframe can be adjusted and the key metrics from there filter the results.

Watch Time

Watch time is a report showing you the total number of minutes your viewers spent watching your material, whether overall or via recording. This is an extremely important consideration as it directly affects the rating on YouTube. If you have a high wait time for your video, you would expect it to be high in the results of the video search.

Average View Duration

The average duration of view (retention rate) is the average amount the viewer is viewing per video. Simply put, if a person watches the first 10 seconds or finishes watching the whole film, it's not the same. The higher that proportion is, the better the likelihood of watching the video by the viewers until the finish. Cards and end screens will help you improve these figures, so if you haven't seen them before, go back here and take care of them.

Traffic Sources

This report will teach you exactly how your audiences explore your online video content. Whether it was the hunt for YouTube, YouTube advertising, recommended footage, or from an external channel (like your website or Facebook page), this report will show you how most users landed there. This is a very important aspect as it clearly shows you what your content promotion (remember, one target per video?) is going to help you visualize where you see the video and where it actually stands. It helps you to learn what places need to be changed and whether you should consider investing in paid ads to bring more traffic to your website.

Now that you've learned what you're going to do with your photos, it's time to check whether or not they've been shipped. Enable your YouTube Analytics is the first thing you need to do. Just go to www.youtube.com/analytics (please be sure to sign in). After joining, you should see a 28-day success rundown of your videos. The timeline can be modified and the key metrics from there filter the data.

Watch Time

Watch time is a report showing you the total number of minutes your viewers spent watching your material, whether overall or via recording. This is an extremely important consideration as it directly affects the rating on YouTube. If you have a high wait time for your video, you would expect it to be high in the results of the video search.

Average View Duration

The average duration of view (retention rate) is the average percentage your audience watches per view. Simply put, if a person watches the first 10 seconds or finishes watching the whole film, it's not the same. The higher this percentage is, the higher your audience's chances of watching the video until the end. Cards and end screens will help you improve these figures, so if you haven't seen them already, go back here and take care of them.

Traffic Sources

This report will teach you exactly how your audiences discover your online video content. Whether it was the hunt for YouTube, YouTube advertising, recommended footage, or from an external channel (like your website or Facebook page), this article would show you how most users landed there. This is a very important tool because it tells you precisely what marketing strategy works best and where you need to spend more time and money.

Demographics

The study on demographics will give you a clear view of what age group is most viewing the posts. Then you can divide these categories by geography or ethnicity to better understand your demographic and see if your YouTube followers fit your already defined customer profile, or if you need to change your targets or videos to help reach your target audience.

Engagement Reports

Such reports will inform you what your audience is most interested in. Here, the most watched, posted, supported, or discussed videos can be found. The report will also show you how your cards and end screens work so that you can automate your videos further.

ADVERTISING ON YOUTUBE

You have done all you could and yet the results from YouTube Analytics aren't as fulfilling as you expected. Okay, I hate breaking it to you, but it won't be easy as sharing it on social media and embedding it on your website and crossing your fingers. You have to take some serious action to pay the bill for a high YouTube ranking. This means you have to advertise on YouTube.

TYPES OF YOUTUBE ADS

You can invest in three different types of YouTube ads. Read on to pick the one that best suits your needs and budget:

1. TrueView Ads

TrueView Ads are the norm you see on YouTube videos and the most popular ads. You simply pay for TrueView ads if the user views the ad for at least 30 seconds, or if, for example, they interact with it by clicking on a call-to-action. Such commercials can be skipped, which ensures that if the user doesn't want to watch them, they can press the' Skip' button on the right, choose not to watch the commercial, so you won't pay a penny for it. Such skippable advertisements can last between 12 seconds and 6 minutes anywhere.

There are two sections of skippable TrueView ads:

- **Video Discovery Ads**

Video Discovery, or previously called In-Display Ads, is the ads that appear on the result pages of the video search, on the homepage of YouTube, and as related videos. A show ad banner will appear on the right after the user clicks to watch the video.

- **In-Stream Ads**

In-Stream advertisements are the ads that appear in the video and play before the user actually gets the chance to watch the video that has been picked. Typically, if they are not involved, audiences have the option to skip the ad after 5 seconds of playing. Such advertisements are ideal for advertisers because with the possibility to include various call-to-action buttons they can be conveniently personalized.

2. Preroll Ads

Although they are legally non-skippable in-stream ads, preroll ads are advertisements that cannot be missed by audiences and that occur before, after, or even mid-roll images. Such preroll advertisements can last from 15-20 seconds and are most effective if they are produced with CTAs to maximize the interest of the audience that you have for such short seconds. Your job here is to create a captivating ad that allows people to click on the ad to get something free (such as signing up for a demo product or an event).

3. Bumpers

Bumpers are the shortest type of ads on YouTube. They're only 6 seconds short and, to be truthful, they aren't the perfect way to tell a story, but if you're looking for a quick way to illustrate your new product or event's launch, they can be of great value. Make sure you carefully use these few seconds and include only the things you want the audience to recall.

Creating Your Ad Campaign

After completion of your marketing video, the next move is to build the advertisement to promote your YouTube clip. To get started, go to Google AdWords account (register if you don't have one) and let's create the campaign:

Type –click the' + Campaign ' button and select' Video' to select your campaign type.

Name –Enter your campaign's name here.

Ad format–Choose the video ad type. Choose' In-stream or video discovery ads,' for example.

Budget–Set the amount of money you want to spend every day. You can also pick the delivery method here, which means you can choose to show the video ads equally during that day (standard delivery), or you can choose to rapidly push views (accelerated delivery).

Networks–You can choose where to view your video ads. You have two options:

- YouTube Videos: Such advertisements can play videos in front of or mid-roll.

- YouTube Search: The ad will appear on the homepage of YouTube, the highlights of the video search and the accompanying column of the site.

Make sure you create different strategies to measure success independently and more efficiently for these two networks.

Locations–For example, you can only select California, United States, to filter the location of the users you want the ad to be shown. You also have the luxury of excluding those locations.

Language, device& Mobile Bidding–This is a great option for determining the network, mobile carrier, and operating system for a more competitive targeting. If the video is shown on a mobile device, you can also reduce or increasing your bid.

Advanced Settings–You can set the start and end date of your campaign in this area, restrict the regular views, build a calendar, etc. This allows you to tailor your ad and get the most return.

Creating the Creative Video Ad–Once you have called your ad category, you can also add the link to the YouTube video for which you want the ad to be played. You then choose to display the ad as an in-display or as an in-stream ad.

Bidding–Choose the maximum price for each ad view you want to pay.

Targeting–Clearly identify the target and ensure that people who want to engage with the ad have opinions. You may aim by age, class, place, value, status of parent, etc.

Advanced Targeting–It helps you to target your viewers with specific keywords or even links that you want to screen your ad.

Linking–Eventually, if you haven't already done so, connect your Google AdWords account to your YouTube channel, press' Full' and launch your campaign.

CHAPTER 5

INSTAGRAM

If you still think about Instagram as the social media platform where you share your selfies and well-plated food from the restaurant, you need to change your mind right now. Okay, I confess, that's what Instagram was when it launched in October 2010. Fast forward to2019, and you see a site full of useful business tools. If you want to successfully sell the company online, you certainly need to have a good Instagram account.

Instagram has over 800 million active monthly users, but the fact that Instagram users are not only involved, they are committed is the main reason why you should choose to know this site inside out and want to have a marketing presence there.

Instagram is all about the visual, and if you happen to be in the business of ecommerce, well, marketing your brand on Instagram may just hit the jackpot.

SETTING UP YOUR INSTAGRAM BUSINESS ACCOUNT

You first need to have an Instagram account up and running to set up your Instagram business page. To do so, you'll need to access the Instagram app.

You'll have two choices when you open the app: login with Facebook, or sign up with an email or phone. To this effect, ensure that your Instagram profile is not connected to your personal Facebook page, use a business email.

Please enter your details after that. Write your company name under Full Name, and write down the unique name for your Instagram profile under Username that will be familiar so that people can find it quickly and interact with the content.

First, add your Instagram profile picture. Is the store's logo or image, the key point is to make the picture simple and recognizable.

Now that you have an Instagram account, making it a business one is the next move. It will need to be connected to a Facebook business page in order for your site to be a business account. If you've taken care of that already, open your Instagram profile. Tap in the upper right corner of the 'Settings' icon. Go to 'Continue to Change to Business Profile' to link to your Facebook page once there. Keep in mind that you need to set your profile to public, so make sure you don't pick the' Personal' alternative.

Your Facebook page should be treated as an alternative there. Tap on 'Start As' to pick it. Tap 'Next'.

Once you're ready, you will be asked for some business info such as location, phone number, and email address. This is crucial to get in touch with your clients, so make sure the relevant information is entered. Click the' Done' button and this is it.

Optimizing Your Profile

Congrats. Now you're a proud owner of a business account from Instagram. But wait until you think you have what it takes to jump straight for your content to be posted. There are a few more steps to take to make your profile look professional and, most likely, appealing to your audience.

Instagram is all about the picture, as mentioned earlier. Which means it should be a good reflection of your name, but it should also provide a consistent visual presence at the same time.

- **The Color Scheme**

Your color scheme for Instagram should be consistent and have a kind of pattern. The colors should go together seamlessly and give a good feeling, whatever you go for the dark and cold or the warm and bright feed.

- **The Lighting**

The lighting is also a crucial element for the esthetic, just like the paint. If you don't know what I mean, think for a second about your own publication. Whatever the subject, the good lighting holds everything together and gives an elegant look.

- **Evenly Spaced-Out Content**

In addition to lighting and shading, the way the images are laid out is also an important ingredient to make your Instagram profile creatively pleasing. The main thing to do is to put the feed together. Try not to clump a lot of busy pictures together, but find a balance for a beautiful and attractive look between them and the sparse ones.

- **Have Consistent Editing**

Another important thing to keep in mind when you actually start posting the images is that they need a consistent style of editing. Of course, you don't have to use just one filter, just try to look more unified by keeping the theme the same so your pictures can blend.

WRITING YOUR BIO

The Instagram bio is by far the most under-used part of Instagram profiles, but that doesn't mean it doesn't matter. In reality, it is quite the contrary. If you're a business that wants to advertise your products or services on Instagram, it's so much more than just an opportunity to have an eye-catching bio that will show the brand to customers.

But it won't just write your name, website, and address. In a fast concise and equally creative way, you will need to write down what your company is and what you are doing. It's time to stand out and let people know what's making your brand better than others like it. Include this in your documents if you have a certain device or service that makes you stand out.

You also need to include #hashtags in your profile. Your profile username and hashtags from your bio are now clickable links due to an update that occurred in 2018. These will become a hyperlink that will carry the viewers to another website by including' #' and' @' before the words. It's pretty good to promote the brand, right?

Take a final look and see if you're satisfied with the way you've delivered the company to the public once you've set up everything.

TYPES OF INSTA POSTS

If everything looks good, it's time for Instagram to post your content. But let's look at the different types of posts you can share on your Instagram profile before you do that:

- **Images**

Instagram's most common type of post is the photo message. Keep in mind that it is important to share a variety of images when posting your brand on Instagram. In this way, you can demonstrate the versatility of your brand and encourage your audience to connect in many ways with your content.
One thing you need to understand when posting pictures is that your viewer (especially the Instagram crowd) is searching for real images, not sales pitches and advertisements. Then you might wonder how to advertise your goods. Try to focus on creating a real-life post, not just sharing images of the product. For example, if you're selling clothes, try to post a picture of a model wearing the shirt with stunning background scenery instead of taking a photo of your newest shirt.

- **Behind-the-Scenes Posts**

This is perhaps the most valued form of message. Posting from behind the scenes allows your audience to take a look at how your company is doing things and get a sense of the atmosphere. For example, on a busy day, you can share a photo showing your employees at work.
Reality is the secret for these posts. To catch the customer's attention, the post needs to look genuine and not fake.

- **Reposts from Employees**

Looking for an original posting method? How about reposting any great content already posted by your employees? Reposting photos from your employees ' Instagram accounts (and, of course, marking them) is a great way to make the brand look a little more' real' and boost your profile's originality. You will thus convey to your viewers that your team has a special bond that will inspire them to participate.

- **Motivational Posts**

Motivational posts contain simple pictures with an uplifting quotation or other motivational text. But as much as these posts will motivate you to improve your brand's reputation, they can sound cheesy and artificial if not performed with good taste. Sparingly sample them to feel more original.

- **Influencer Posts**

Influencer posts are the posts posted by a celebrity or other well-known person with a large base of followers. If you sell nutritious and organic drinks, for example, you might want to ask an athlete or a successful fitness mentor to post a picture of them drinking one of your smoothies. The idea here is to reach out to the followers and some of the fans of the influencer. When can I do it? Find and contact the inquiry with an influencer, offering something back. For free samples, many of them will do it, but others may ask for money in return.

- **Educational Posts**

Those posts that give quick tips on how something can be accomplished or made are considered instructional posts. These can either be images or photos, but the main thing is these provide simple instructions that can be followed by the viewer to accomplish something.

- **User-Generated Content**

While workplace reposts meant posting images and videos uploaded by your staff, user-generated content would mean curating messages that your followers viewed. Not only will you decide to share a post from a customer make your day, but it will also show your other fans that you really care for your customers. Just make sure the original image or video is credited and the poster is tagged.

- **Newsjacking**

Newsjacking includes holiday posts that are popular. Yet I'm not even talking about the big holidays like Thanksgiving or Valentine's Day. There's a holiday for almost everything, so you might want to consider getting into your spirit and exchanging happy wishes for those carefree hours.

TAKING QUALITY IMAGES

Now that you've discovered what kind of photos you should upload on Instagram, let's see how to actually post attractive ones that will catch your audience's attention and make them click and comment on the ' like ' icon.

First of all, follow the rules for the image size:

- Square Images – 1080 x 1080 pixels
- Landscape Images – 1080 x 566 pixels
- Profile Images – 1350 x 1080 pixels

- **The Rule of Thirds**

Moving the subject from the center and creating a photo imbalance is a very popular and attractive technique that most photographers enjoy using. Called the third party law, the fans would enjoy this strategy.

Make sure the grid lines on your camera are turned on for quick video loading.

- **Single Subject Is the Key**

Posting messy images will not catch the eye of your follower as it will be easy and ordered. If shooting photos, seek to focus on a single subject. That means cropping out of the picture and getting rid of unnecessary things, blurring the extra subject, or shooting against a plain, transparent backdrop.

- **Say Yes to the Negative Space**

Negative space is a term for your subject's empty space. Shooting with a lot of negative space is just what you need in terms of selling a single product. So, the attention of your follower will be drawn anywhere you want it to be – on your commodity.

- **Take Advantage of Different Perspective**

From an eye level we people see the world around us. To this effect, professional photographers usually take images from a different perspective and use different angles to make the shot look as natural as possible.

- **Play with Patterns and Symmetry**

Whether a wooden table or a tiled floor, choose an enticing pattern that your subject can disturb. Try to break the third party rule from time to time and add some balance to your pictures by putting your focus in the center of the design you have selected.

- **Natural Light is Your Friend**

Natural light in photography works best. Seek not to overshadow your subject by standing above the scenery, but by aiming outside or next to a window you tend to take advantage of the natural light.

VIDEOS
It can be posted to Instagram as long as the footage is 60 seconds or less.

- **Boomerangs**

Boomerang is an Instagram environment that enables you to capture 3-second videos that can play back and forth. You can quickly post a Boomerang to Instagram by clicking the camera icon on Instagram and choosing the' Boomerang' option. Boomerangs are a fun way of highlighting happy situations like skipping or high-fiving.
Through mixing images for a boring and fun film, you can also create a Boomerang.

- **Hyperlapse**

Instagram hyperlapse is a tool that allows you to shorten your long videos and convert them into material that can be posted on Instagram. Download the Hyperlapse software and you can record, save and share your own time-lapse images.

- **Instagram Live**

Instagram also offers the option to share live content, just like Facebook Live. If you're interested in this way getting in touch with your customers, just open your Instagram camera, select the'Live' setting, then just hit the' Start Live Video ' button. Before you launch your live video stream, you will receive a notification from all of your followers who are currently online. You can also engage your live audience in real time by commenting on your live video, which is a great opportunity for a Q&A session with your customers in real time.

- **IGTV**

Instagram's latest video feature is IGTV or Instagram TV. This is a way to watch longer vertical videos for Instagram fans, which can also be useful for your marketing strategy if you were talking about including any longer videos or even some interviews.

IGTV can be downloaded from your App Store either through the Instagram app or through your own IGTV app. Though, if you're thinking about streaming on IGTV, you'll need to download the app and create a channel there. You can then upload videos from 15 seconds to 10 minutes in length online. You can run your videos for up to an hour if you have a verified account. On your mobile, you can only use IGTV, as this site is not yet available via your desktop computer.
Keep in mind that Instagram Live is not the same. IGTV is already recorded and uploaded, allowing you to finish and edit the video as long as you want.

- **Instagram Stories**

Instagram stories is a very popular feature that is essentially a workaround for over-posting on Instagram. It's basically a way for you to post regularly on Instagram, but without your primary feed getting compromised.

In comparison to your filtered images, this is a time-sensitive option that reveals a touch of raw feel. It's much more genuine than the usual posts, which is why the followers highly appreciate it.

There are three options to share your Instagram story:
- Click the camera icon in the top left corner
- Enter the' Your Story +' button above your feed
- And just swipe right to open your app with your cursor.

You can add text or even include a GIF, audio, a venue, and a lot of other fun features as well. And the best part of that? Instagram actually allows you to add another Instagram account in your post, so it's a great way to connect with a similar business, a team member, or you can use this option to tag a customer directly to thank for the help.

Simply press the' Your Story+ ' button to print, or you can just choose to save and update the story later when it's more convenient for you. At the top of your main feed you can find your story as well as through your profile picture.

WRITING EYE-CATCHING CAPTIONS

Although it is the picture that first catches the viewer's eye, if the caption below is less than impressive, it will not inspire the viewers to engage with it. But how to compose amazing subtitles? To avoid getting confused by finding the right words, follow these simple tips below.

- **Take Your Time**

Okay, for your book, you're not writing a line. You don't really need days to brainstorm the perfect line that will accompany your new picture, but it can certainly help you to write a few drafts and ask your friends and family's opinion. Your posts ' main purpose is to engage users, particularly with the new Instagram algorithm. The top posts they see when they visit the Instagram app are the ones that Instagram feels they'll find the most entertaining. That ought to be a good reason for you to find the time to create captions that wow your audience.

- **The Beginning Counts the Most**

Instagram supports 2,200 characters in the captions, which is nice if you equate this site to Facebook, where you can't post more than 140 characters. Bear in mind, however, that your audience won't see the entire text on their phones. Only the first few lines are shown; the audience needs to press the' Further' button to read the rest of the letter. To get your audience hooked, if you really want to tell a story people are actually reading, make the first few lines as attention-grabbing as possible.
There's no excuse you're afraid to get into specifics and write longer captions as long as you're writing killer beginnings. But, if you want the rest of the chat to your viewers, shorter captions would work best.

- **Engage**

I don't can't to be seem to emphasize this enough, but the key to successful marketing is ENGAGEMENT. Otherwise, you're just another company that sells to people unimportant stuff. Make sure to always include a call-to-action in your captions to inspire your audience to participate, and invite your audience to like, share, and comment on your story.

- **Work on Your Instagram Voice**

Remember how we said that for each platform you need a different approach? For each of your social media profiles, your voice should be distinctive. For Facebook, what promotes the brand on LinkedIn probably won't work. Your Instagram posts should be carefree, optimistic, and written with a distinctive sound that your client would remember over time. Play words, colors, emojis, and other innovative resources to give the brand a distinct feel.

- **Their Majesty, (#Hashtags)**

You probably already know what hashtags are unless you're new to social media and not current on the internet. These are the keyword phrases that are written together, without gaps, and boldly have before them the' #' symbol. Despite being born on Instagram, hashtags have now taken over social media entirely.

Why are you trying to use hashtags? Because they will help your posts get seen, and given that Instagram publishes more than 80 million images every day, do you see how valuable it is, right? Get it correctly, and it will reach the viewers in no time.

There are three ways your audience can see tagged content on Instagram:

- First, they see their TOP 9 posts, which are tagged posts that Instagram thinks the user will most likely want to engage with

- Most RECENT 9 posts showing tagged posts displayed in chronological order

- RELATED hashtags showing similar hashtags that people use to discuss that or a related topic.

To ensure you can broaden your post's reach, use a few additional related hashtags to help your audience notice the photo. Of example, you may want to add hashtags like #vegan, #healthysnack, or #matchapowder if you want to tag your picture with #smoothie. The aim is to tag a few additional details to clarify your photo's theme.

Note: In order to display your tagged posts on the hashtag lists, your account must be PUBLIC.

Finding the Right Hashtag
But what if you are unable to determine which hashtags to use? That can also be easily solved, as searching hashtags within the Instagram app is the simplest way to do that. Were you thinking of a hashtag? Only type your favorite hashtag into Instagram's 'Search Bar', filter the search results into Tags, and see how many posts the hashtag was used, see similar hashtags, and suggest some appropriate keyword phrases.
Would you like to increase your reach? Why not put in your article some trending hashtags and mix them with your keywords to make the post more relevant?

Formatting Your Hashtag
Now that you have found the perfect hashtag for your post, you have to decide how to use it. There, the main rule is to be human. The hashtags used are meant to have a rhythm and go well together. Read your post aloud and see how it sounds before clicking 'Post'. Looks like spammy? Don't be scared! Even if you can't include your hashtags in the post as you want them to, you can always choose to place them at the end of your post, or even at the start. We will do the same job irrespective of where they are.
Note: An average of 2.5 hashtags per post is used by businesses. In order to keep your audience interested, try to limit your hashtags and never include more than 4, to avoid seemingly trying too hard.

MARKETING YOUR BRAND

Approaching Instagram without a proper marketing strategy is the biggest mistake you can make. If you don't have a perfectly crafted approach, it won't be enough to share high quality content with the right hashtags. Being a unique platform for social media, Instagram needs to promote its own distinctive style. Read on to see what you can do with this platform to help the business expand.

Know Your Audience

The only way to ensure that you market the brand to the right people and expect interest in return is to know exactly who your target is. You can use that audience if you are already selling your goods on other social media platform, but keep in mind the Instagram community is a bit different.

Spend some time tracking the hashtags linked to your brand and the products / services you offer to find your perfect Instagram following. Find out the users who use these hashtags, and find out their accounts. Take note of the characteristics that identify the ideal customer and create a perfect audience.

Analyze

You're just beginning your marketing journey on Instagram, which means you can't be exactly sure what works and what the audience doesn't appreciate. Spend some time peeking into the accounts of your peers to get a clear picture of what posts get the highest dedication and what pictures remain ignored. See their results and take notes of the things that have been most effective in reaching the audience. Wasn't it after all Picasso who said the great artists were stealing? I'm not, of course, concerned about copyright infringement, but using their accounts as advice on what to post and when to communicate with your fans.

Post When Your Audience is Active the Most

When you search on Google "what is the right time to post on Instagram," you can find a number of pages all displaying recent statistics based on millions of updates and user engagement. The latest ones specifically say the best time to post the material is between 9 a.m. and 11 a.m. EST. But that doesn't mean it's the time when the audience of YOUR brand is most active.

You will find the perfect time to post for your company in many respects. Monitoring your audience and taking notes when the most active time zones are different, as well as tracking the progress of your posts over time, are both great indicators. But if you're searching for the most trouble-free option, then it's probably the best choice to download some algorithms that will measure this automatically for you.

If you don't like any of these choices, it can also be successful to adhere to 9am-11am law. Consider other factors that are also important to your business. For example, if your crowd is made up of adolescents and young adults, avoid posting early in the morning.

Schedule Your Posts

Once you find out what the perfect time is for your business to post, make sure that your posts are actually shared. The best way to make sure the latest ones say the best time for sharing your content is between 9 am and 11 am EST. But that doesn't mean it's the moment when the market of YOUR brand is most involved.

You will find the perfect time to post for your company in many respects. Monitoring the followers and taking notes when the most popular time zones are different, as well as monitoring the success of your posts over time, are both excellent markers. But if you're looking for the most trouble-free option, then it's probably the best choice to download some algorithms that will calculate this automatically for you.

If you don't like any of these options, it can also be productive to stick to 9am-11am rule. Remember certain considerations that are also important to your company. For example, if your crowd is made up of adolescents and young adults, avoid posting early in the morning.

Schedule Your Posts

When you figure out what the perfect time is for your company to publish, make sure that your updates are actually shared. The best way to make sure the article doesn't slip your mind and is posted at the right time is to plan it.

Simply write down your post and open the menu at the bottom of your screen. Choose 'Publish on Scheduled Date' online, pick your chosen date and time, and wait for Instagram to take care of the rest. For this function, if you're too busy, you can also use a scheduling feature where you can write a few posts in advance and plan the date and time that you want them to be written. Www.sendible.com and www.later.com both have excellent Instagram profile management tools.

Be Consistent

While we've discussed this before, consistency is the key. Your brand must first be reliable on Instagram to be effective. And I'm not just thinking about the article. Consistency will extend across your post, from your profile colors to the arrangement of your images. The easiest way to catch your attention and attract new fans is to learn what the essence of your brand is and change the content to suit it.

ATTRACTING FOLLOWERS

Each of the below tactics will help you gain followers on Instagram, there are a few tricks you need to get up your sleeve to boost your fan base and get a few more likes.

- **Become a Follower**

The next thing you need to do is start following profiles, hoping that your name and bio are written in a compelling way, that your profile is configured as mentioned before, and that you have already started posting quality content. Sharing similar accounts and some other business-related passions will help you become part of a community that could throw your way to many followers. Once you begin to follow people and businesses, Instagram will also propose other related accounts you can become a fan of.

But don't allow that to end there. Start to interact with their content when you become their follower. Not only will this spread your brand awareness, it will also humanize it, which people greatly appreciate.

- ### Ask for Interaction

Asking people to spread the word is a great marketing tactic that may need more effort, but always pays off. Start and get them to share your page with your friends and family to invite their followers to become your followers. Please contact brand ambassadors and ask them to share the content you post with other similar accounts that may allow you to expand your number of followers. Seek not to be pushy and send something in return at all times. It always seems that free samples and generous discounts do the trick.

It can be quite beneficial to work with an influencer. You will 'borrow' some of their fans by letting the influencer support your goods and bring more traffic to your page.

- ### Go with Instagram Stories

Use Instagram Stories to increase the brand's visibility. How? In addition to being a great tool to help you reach your new fans, Instagram Stories can also expand your number of followers when they surface on the Instagram Search page. This means they can still locate your Instagram Stories from the Discover tab while looking for something specific, even if someone isn't your fan.

- **Promote**

Similar to Facebook and YouTube, sharing your Instagram profile on your website and other social media platforms is the shortest, but sometimes the best, way to attract new followers on Instagram.

TURNING FOLLOWERS INTO CUSTOMERS

It can be perfect for your business to have a lot of Instagram followers. But if those users just press the' Like' button and your link to them will end there, your marketing strategy will most likely go up in flames. The trick is not to attract as many fans as possible, but to make them clients. Here are a few things that can help you inspire your supporters to take action:

- **Promotions**. People love ads and first-time deals on Instagram. Limited deals and special offers may attract your followers to give your brand an opportunity to see what you're selling. Also note to highlight the importance of quick action and mention a set date so that your fans can take the plunge as quickly as possible.

- **Charity**. Looking for a way more millennials can be attracted? How about setting some of your income back and donating it to a charity? Studies show that over 80% of millennials expect firms to make generous donations, so try to live up to their expectations. In addition to building affection for your brand, this way you can also include your supporters and support a very important cause. That could make them yours ' long-term clients.

- **Contests**. Contests are the perfect way for people to try their products. Make it a requirement for individuals to follow your account or even post to enter the contest by naming your name.

- **Teasers**. Posting teasers of your new products is the best way to allow the followers to see what you're working on quickly. Combine your teasers with restricted discounts and allow people to buy a special price for your sweet, new product.

- **Live launches**. Instagram Live presents you with a great opportunity to reveal your new products live. This will promote interaction with your consumers as this choice gives them the opportunity to ask you in real time any questions about the product.

WHAT ABOUT ANALYTICS?

I hate to disappoint you, but Facebook and YouTube don't have an analytics platform like the built-in ones. Fingers crossed, this will be changed for the better soon. That doesn't mean you can't chart your progress with Instagram, though. Below are some tips to help you calculate the growth of your brand on Instagram and get a clear picture of the success of your market.

First of all, once you switch to a Business Account, Instagram offers some limited tools like measuring your followers ' growth, commitment, organic reach, etc. By clicking on the' View Insights ' button just below your photos and videos, you can access this tool.

If you're looking for a more in-depth way to track your Instagram metrics, then buying a third-party tool that will enable you to more effectively measure your performance is probably a good choice. https:/pro.iconosquare.com/ is a great tool for managing this. Their pricing varies from € 29 to € 79 per month, depending on your plan and commitment, but the best part is that they offer you a 14-day free trial to see what they can do for your marketing strategy and decide if the investment is worth it.

For some Instagram measurements, you can also go to the Facebook Ad Manager, but bear in mind that this choice is quite narrow and not for every post or campaign.

ADVERTISING ON INSTAGRAM

Once you become active on Instagram, to increase your traffic and get more shares, you need to consider investing in advertising your content there. If you're familiar with Facebook advertisements, you already have halfway through Instagram marketing, as the setup and budgeting of your Insta advertisement is actually done by Facebook.

You must claim your Instagram Business account and connect it to your Facebook page to start the process.

Pick your favorite editor (Advertising Administrator, Facebook Ads API or Power Editor) after you take care of that. With social media marketers, the Ads Manager is the most popular, so you might want to choose that tool.

The next move is to pick your ad goal. You'll see there are quite a few choices, but these are the ones you need to choose from for Instagram advertising:

- Brand Exposure
- Engagement
- Impact• Traffic
- Conversions

- App Installs
- Video Views

So call your ad package and target your market. You will have to set a lot of variables, such as age, place, class, actions, job, etc. And, if you have one, you can also pick a specific audience that was previously created.

Instead, under the specified platforms, pick the' Edit Placement ' option and click on' Instagram.' This is a very important step because you're only going to advertise on Facebook if you don't choose Instagram.

You will then be told to set your budget and plan your advertising. Complete this move as discussed earlier and go ahead with setting up your materials. You can either choose to raise an existing post or add a new photo or video to display as an advertising, there are two choices for you here.

Simply click the 'Place Order' button once all is sorted, and that's it. Your ad campaign for Instagram is ready to run. Just be sure to report your results and keep track of the success of your ad. For this reason, you will find the metrics either in the Advertising Manager of Facebook or in the marketing app, if you   use   one.

CHAPTER 6

TWITTER

Twitter is definitely a great forum for your company with about 6,000 new tweets per second. Whatever your ambitions may be, your target audience is sure to be reflected by a huge chunk of the 326 million monthly active Twitter accounts. With that in mind, it is safe to say that you can consider selling your brand on Twitter a very lucrative tactic for you. But it won't be enough to just sign up and tweet. You also need a well-crafted marketing strategy for Facebook, just like any other social media platform. The chapter will help you learn how to promote the brand on Twitter and figure out how to hide behind Larry the duck.

How is Twitter Different?

We have already addressed the importance of having a different approach to your networks in social media. For your Twitter profile, what works for Facebook may not work for it. Yet Twitter is really the one that stands out when it comes to social media platforms.

In comparison to Facebook or Pinterest, Twitter does not rely on web broadcasting. Rather, Twitter is all about user-to-user interaction and contact, whether ordinary people, corporations or even government officials.

- Sharing knowledge
- Branding
- Driving engagement
- Interacting with clients
- Reputation management

- Networking

Twitter is the site that thrives off the connection. It's special this way. Because it is not a website whose main purpose is to access and distribute content. People usually go on Twitter to become part of a conversation and connect with the content, not watching videos or browsing through images.

CREATING YOUR TWITTER PROFILE

If you're just a person who's curious in what the leaders of the world have to say next, you can just sign up, post (or not) a video, and start retweeting. But if you're a company and want to advertise your products on Twitter, you need a profile that's in-depth and carefully built.

To create a Twitter account for your business, follow these next few steps:

- Go to www.twitter.com.
- Click on the button 'Sign Up'.
- Enter and click' Build my account' in the required information.
- You'll be asked by Twitter to support 5 users when you press 'Next' on your homepage. Make sure they're in some way related to your business.
- At this stage you can choose to add contacts from your email address, but this is an optional step. Your account for Twitter is now being established.

Tap on'Edit Profile' to go to your password. The first thing you need to do is upload your profile pic, which is normally your logo or some other picture of your brand for company.

The Bio

Unfortunately, to show your company to the Twitter community, you only get 160 characters. On the plus side, this gives you the chance to be really imaginative, choose your words carefully, and say only the things that matter most.

Just like on Facebook, YouTube, and Instagram, the bio on Twitter of your company should also include important keywords to help your customer find you better. Keep in mind that followers should be appealing, optimistic, and draw. It seems that fun bios works for the audience like a magnet, so you might want to add a humorous line to catch a few more eyes.

The Optimization

Your bio is important, but if your whole profile is not carefully designed, then the trick will not be accomplished by humorous lines and appropriate keywords. Your profile should not only be able to attract potential customers visually, but should also be able to encourage them to start a conversation about the products or services that you offer.

Add a professional profile image reflecting the company (like your branding or storefront) and add a high-quality header picture complementing the profile image; talk about an upcoming event or the new offering.

When your exterior is friendly to the eye, take advantage of hashtags and emojis, and make sure you post material that is important to your audience.

The Verification

It's an important aspect to get verified on Twitter. A checked profile means you're the real deal and the followers can have faith in you. It can be of great value for your business to have the blue checkmark next to your account name, so make sure you check your profile right from the start.

Let People Know

Remember that your profile is not only up and running, it's time to show it off, but also ready for success. Whether you're on your website, other social media platforms, signing an email or adding it to your store's front window, letting people know about your Twitter handling is the best strategy to boost your followers list.

THE RIGHT MARKETING STRATEGY

Marketing your Twitter brand goes far beyond setting up the right way for your profile. It's the right mix of activities that will boost your brand's promotion process and bring you more customers in turn. But to do so, it is important to schedule and carefully organize these marketing-oriented practices. Here's how you can power-pack the brand's operation on Twitter:

- **Listen and Take Notes**

If people think about ads (whether on social media or not), they usually consider investing money. And while it's true that the more you spend, the better the likelihood of returns, the key tactic is often glossed over when it comes to promoting the brand. The first step is to see exactly where you (and your competition) are standing before reaching your wallet. And since we're talking about ads on Twitter, the first move is to test how committed people are to your company.

The very first thing you need to do is to test what your company is being addressed by the audience on Twitter. What people are most interested in? What do they think you need to improve? What aren't they pleased with? Understanding this can help you smash the competition and gain direct customer feedback.

Here are some items you need to listen to on Twitter:

- Name of your company
- Name of your goods and services

- Competition
- Slogans of your brand
- Few word of mouth in your business
- Name of your CEO or other members
- Names of promotions
- Other keywords

Take note of things relevant to your brand and incorporate them into your other marketing act.

- **Create Great Content**

That goes without saying, but basically sharing great content is what attracts the viewer, encourages them to retweet, share, and connect with your brand. You only have 280 characters, so you're expected to be picky with your vocabulary and say only the things that are most important to your brand and are sure to resonate with your Twitter followers.

Be Helpful. Beyond listening to what they have to say or personally communicating with them, it's great to show the fans that by supporting them in some way you care for their needs and interests. Sharing a trending post that will benefit your market is a great way to get your consumers noticed more. If you can't find one, visit the 'TrendSpottr' app to access and explore any emerging trends.

Use #Hashtags. I have said this too many times, but when it comes to Twitter ads, hashtags are the single most important thing. You can also compose in your notebook without them, not post the content online. What's the reason? Because it's the hashtags that make sure people find and share your content.

Be Conversational. Making Twitter one-dimensional is a violation in advertisement in the social media. Your Tweets should not only be broadcasts, but should open the door to interaction and conversation:
- Ask questions from your audience
- Make sure that at least 30 percent of your Tweets are replies

- Don't just tweet links; make sure you include a line of your own thoughts as well as
- Make sure you tweet your audience directly.

• Plan Ahead

You should be present at all times. This means you have to get into the mood for every holiday and special event. You will continue with your Christmas tweets as you roll in late November. Come mid-January, you need to decorate your Twitter profile with tweets from your Valentine. Check the latest trends and don't hesitate to use the best hashtags for #Holiday.

• Post at the Right Time

You should always be there. This ensures that for every celebration and special event, you have to get into the mood. When you roll late November, you can start with your Christmas tweets. You need to decorate your Twitter profile with your Valentine's tweets in mid-January. Check the latest developments and feel free to use #Holiday's top hashtags.

Tweet Regularly. Once a day tweeting is a great way to stay active and take part in the hottest conversations. You will try to post more, but keep your eyes open and see how your Twitter presence will be affected. So you can find the pace for your company that works best.

Stick to the Best Practice. The best times to post on Twitter are 12 pm, 5 pm, and 6 pm. It, of course, depends on your audience, so it is advised to try and evaluate here again to see what suits you best.

Schedule Your Tweets. When you determine the best hours for sharing your content, plan your tweets to make sure you get the most attention to each of your tweets.

Twitter Video

While Twitter isn't the first thing that comes to mind when it comes to promoting the brand through video content, statistics say the Twitter audience is also very involved in digesting videos.

While sharing videos from Twitter, there are a few options available:

- First, you can use the native functionality on Twitter to capture and share up to 140 seconds directly.
- Another choice is to use a live streaming application called Periscope (owned by Twitter) that blends into your profile and guarantees your followers see your live stream. When recording is finished, the viewers will have access to the video.

Thread Tweets Together

Do you want to provide content in an organized matter? Try to combine threading tweets. This facility allows you to start a tweet and then add more tweets to the original by simply threading them to the first tweet. This is a perfect way to tell a story or keep alive an ongoing conversation, without content anywhere.

MEASURING THE RESULTS

The best way to evaluate your Twitter success is to measure what your marketing strategy has achieved so far and to determine how much your audience is engaged with your brand. A basic exercise will help you identify your weak spots and weaknesses as well as help you decide how the plan should be improved and what it is worth investing in.

Twitter Analytics

Twitter Analytics is the built-in app to measure your Twitter account's overall performance. Click on your avatar to use Twitter Analytics and then select the 'Analytics' to see your monthly highlights. You can also jump to analytics.twitter.com straight away.

You'll find there:

- Top Tweet–the most impressive tweet for a selected month.
- New Followers–Number of people pressing the' Follow' button for the month in question.
- Top Follower –This is the one with the most followers (including your New Follower).
- Top Mention–A tweet in which a user mentions your brand that gained the most impressions for the month.
- Commits–Anything that people click on (photos, connections, videos, comments, etc.) • Commitment rate–When you split the amount of commits by the number of interactions for a certain post, you get the engagement rate.
- Reaching ratio–This is calculated by dividing the number of tweet views by the total number of followers and indicating how many followers have seen the tweet picked.

Some fantastic resources provided by Twitter Analytics are' Audiences '–where you can gather information about your audience (location, gender, preferences, etc.) and'Ad Campaign Dashboard'–where you'll gain access to your successful promotions result.

ADVERTISING ON TWITTER

If you want to keep your Tweets from getting lost in the popular content whirlpool, then it seems like the smart thing to do is to give them a little push and make sure they're seen by your followers. Twitter advertising will help the right customers receive the post.

Type of Twitter Ads

There are a few ways you can advertise on Twitter:

- **Promoted Posts**

These are posts you pay to make sure you see people who don't already follow you on Twitter. The promoted tweets can also be liked, retweeted, shared, etc., just like regular tweets. The only distinction is in the' Promoted' sign next to them between them and the usual tweets.

- **Promoted Accounts**

Accounts Promoted do not promote your Tweets, rather your Twitter profile. They help you find out more about your page and get you more followers by spreading your Tweeter profile to users who may be interested in your brand but don't follow you now.

- **Promoted phenomena**

Promoted trends are the things that people talk about on Facebook. Promoted trends are an opportunity to endorse your own #hashtag at the top of the most popular trends chart. So when Twitter users browse for a particular trend, they will see a list of verified findings, with your hashtag at the top. This will increase your organic exposure and enhance your followers list.

- **Automated ads**

While personalized Twitter advertisements are a better way to achieve your specific business target, there is another choice for those who are unaware about how much they want to invest, have a limited amount of time or lack a strong team. This alternative is called Promoted Mode for Twitter.

Twitter Promoted Mode is an interactive ad for which you are charged a flat fee. You can automatically promote your first 10 tweets (of the day) to your target audience with a fixed price of $99 (plus tax) per month.

You can expect to reach around 30,000 people with this option, according to Twitter. This will also most likely bring you about 30 new followers every month.

CREATING YOUR AD CAMPAIGN

It's a very straightforward process to create a Twitter advertising program. Just follow the steps below and will be sharing the Tweets.

- **Advertising account**

If you're using Twitter for the first time for ads, you'll need a password. To get going, go to https:/ads.twitter.com/login.

- **The objective**

The ad campaign must be focused on a specific goal for your company, which ensures that this is the stage in which you determine what you want your Twitter advertising to accomplish. Whether you want to reach more followers, build awareness of your brand, increase the rate of engagement or another reason, choose your goal wisely and click 'Next' to continue.

- **Ad group and bidding**

You choose your ad group at this point, which is a sub-category of your campaign. Sticking to a single ad-group is advised at this stage, but as you become more familiar with Twitter ads, you should break it into a few sub-groups to target different markets or play with budgets and timing.

You will also have to choose your budget here, or how much you want to pay for each interaction (video view, engagement, etc.) Click' Next' for the next step when you're all set.

- **Creative and Ad Placement**

Pick from the archive of old tweets the tweet you want to encourage, or simply create a new one here.

- Users ' profiles
- Profiles and comprehensive tweet pages
- Search results

Click 'Next' again.

- **Target Audience**

Here you need to pick your desired audience through several tailored choices. To identify the type of audience you want to endorse your Tweets, you will need to choose venue, gender, age, language, technology, etc. You also have the option of adding your own target audience list (such as your email list) or you can also choose to target users close to the group that is already following you.

- **Launch your business**

Start your campaign and begin your ads, just click on 'Begin Campaign'   and   you   are   done.

CHAPTER 7

LINKEDIN

With more than 562 million members from all over the world, LinkedIn is the largest and most popular professional network. If you want to develop your relationships and grow your network, it is an absolute must for your company to be involved on LinkedIn. It is, after all, the lead generation's largest social network.

LinkedIn, being a website that links companies and experts, requires a unique marketing strategy, of course. The law here is the word of mouth. It's not about whom you know, but whom, through the people you know, you can connect with. But it won't turn out to be a successful marketing campaign to sell your brand through your obsolete personal page. Read on to see how your winning marketing strategy can be developed (and implemented) to get you to the top on LinkedIn.

SETTING UP YOUR LINKEDIN COMPANY PAGE

You need a full-blown business profile for marketing your brand on LinkedIn. The business page is a professional way to let members of LinkedIn know about your name, your products, your organization and the job opportunities provided by your company.

Although the business websites were mainly used as HR landing pages, this website now offers a great opportunity to raise awareness of the brand and market your services to potential clients.

You need an active personal profile on LinkedIn first to set up a company website. If you have one, just follow the next steps to build your company's website.

- **Add your company**

Go to https:/business.linkedin.com/marketing/linkedin accounts and click 'Edit Your Account'. Type your company name and create a URL to help people find your website. Note that later you won't be able to change the URL, so make sure you choose wisely. Then check the checkbox to check that you are the company's official representative and click' Launch Account.'

The shell will be created automatically. Only press the 'Get Started' button to start creating your website.

- **Add your image**

Import your logo (recommended 300x 300 pixels) as your profile image and add a cover image (preferably 1536x 768 px) to give an insight into what your business is about. Keep in mind that logos businesses have more traffic, so don't be tempted to miss this phase.

- **Create Your Description**

LinkedIn allows you to use 2,000 characters for your description, but be aware that it is the first 156 words that are displayed on Google in the preview of your company page, so make sure you write an excellent start.

You have 20 specialties to add. Think of them as keywords advertisements that can help people discover their business on LinkedIn, so be sure to reflect the business ' power and knowledge here.

- **Company details**

Here you enter the location of your company, the URL of your website, your industry, the size and form of your product, as well as other important details identifying your company.

- **Publish the page**

Tap ' Publish' to go online. It is best to see what the business page looks like when other people press on it before you start. Tap ' Member Window' to try it out. If the look of your page is not satisfied, go to' Manage Page' and make some modifications.

- **Page Administrators**

If you're not planning to run your LinkedIn Company page alone, you'll need to select the people you can administer the page.

Tap on the 'Me' button at the top of your screen to add more staff. Go to 'Manage', and then select your Company Page. There, pick the 'Admin Tools' option for 'Web Admins'. Enter the name of the users you want to view the list.

Note: To pick them as admins, you must already be linked to these individuals on LinkedIn.

The Perfect Strategy

Only having a business website doesn't mean you're going to get the right connections. You also need to have a good marketing plan for LinkedIn, just like any other site. Here's what you can do to improve your chances of success:

Create a Showcase Page

Showcase pages are the perfect way to display a particular part of your company you're most proud of. This is a great opportunity to put your best product in the spotlight and attract potential customers.

The view pages act as some kind of subdomains for your business website, and having one can really make a difference because members on LinkedIn can also visit them individually if they are specifically interested in a particular product or service. You can have pages up to view.

Tap the' Me ' button to build one, then pick your Company Page under' Manage.' Then go to' Admin Tools'—' Create a page for a showcase.'

Have Your Employees Connected
Your employees are your biggest advocates on LinkedIn. Having them as followers means you have access to their networks and connections, which can increase your reach significantly and bring more traffic to your company page. Encourage your employees to be connected to your company page to raise awareness of the brand.

Keep Followers Informed
The easiest way to boost your market is to be happy with the one you have. Make sure you write valuable content on your business on a regular basis, such as blogs, blog posts or other updates. Even, if you can conceive of a worthwhile external post for your fans, do not hesitate to publish it as well.

Choose LinkedIn Groups
LinkedIn Groups provide you with a perfect way to connect with people in your immediate circle from your profession. Active in a LinkedIn Community and engaged in conversations will lead to more visits to your Site.

Would you like to find a group that suits your goal? With the 'Group Discover' option, you can check out some suggestions for LinkedIn, or just use the search bar if you know what you're looking for.

Go Global
If you have clients in some countries where English is not the official language, then you may want to consider adding a summary in other languages of your product. Don't worry, for that reason you don't have to find a translator. LinkedIn offers multi-language tools for you to take care of this.

Publish at the Right Times

Like the plans for your other sites, you also need to schedule your LinkedIn posting. Data from LinkedIn says the best time to post material on LinkedIn is in the morning and after business hours. This is when people are most involved, so you may want to take advantage of this knowledge and then plan your message.

ADVERTISING ON LINKEDIN

If you want to direct your message to other practitioners, whether CEOs or influencers, you should definitely take advantage of ads on LinkedIn. You will start with the next steps after you decide what you want to promote and who is your target audience.
- **Your 'Campaign Manager' Account**

First of all, you need to have a' Campaign Manager ' account to take care of here https:/www.linkedin.com/ad-beta/login. This is a tool that gives you the easiest way to manage and automate your advertising. However, this app provides some useful tools to show the output of your ads, so it's an added bonus.
- **Choose the Type of Your Ad**

Next, the type of ad you want to advertise must be selected. Three options are available:
- Sponsored Inmail
- Sponsored content
- Text Ad

With all three forms, you can also build your advertisement to ensure maximum coverage.

Once you choose the ad form, enter your campaign name, select the language of your target audience, and select the call-to-action feature, which is only available for the Sponsored-Content advertisements.

- **Create the Ad**

The best thing about the Campaign Manager is to guide you through the production steps, giving advice and guidance along the way. Follow the steps choosing the most appropriate choices for your target.

- **Target the Ad**

Make sure your ad is aimed at the right people at this point. You may state such requirements such as location, names of classes, company names, degree, job title, class, age, years of experience, qualifications, etc. Make sure that you save your qualifications so that the next time you want to advertise on LinkedIn you can speed things up.

- **Set the Budget and Schedule**

There are three options you can pay for ads:
- Cost per click (CPC)
- Cost per impression (CPM)–for user display messages
- Cost per send–for supported InMail advertising (here you only pay for receiving messages)

For the CPM and CPS alternative, you are allowed to set a maximum daily budget you are willing to spend and a bid price. Just plan the beginning and end date and time for the ad after that, and you're done.

IS YOUR MARKETING STRATEGY WORKING?

When you take your stats from another social media platform, the real picture of your LinkedIn success is probably missing. Checking out the built-in analytics tool on LinkedIn is the best way to check whether your marketing strategy works.

Go to the top of your screen toolbar fount and press the' Analytics' tab. You can see that there are three options available:

- **Visitors**-This is where data is stored on the people visiting your website. Here you can see a general overview of page views, user stats, you can separate data from a certain time and date, see data from different sites on your site, and see detailed information about users visiting your page (job feature, venue, sector, etc.)

- **Feedback**–here you can find information about the content you post. Such indicators of communication include views, downloads, shares, comments, taps, etc.

- **Followers**–You can review your list of supporters in more depth in the' Followers' tab.

CHAPTER 8

7 SOCIAL MEDIA MARKETING STRATEGIES

If you call them tactics, behaviors, or just a form of social media marketing, there are some items you need to take care of to dust off your lonely business social web. And, if your company is new to the social media world, establish a good process that will make your business standout.

1. Set Your Scheme and Stick to It

Probably your posts and tweets will go unnoticed if you don't have a thought-out strategy. In addition to your goals, which should already be set firmly, you also need to have a good course of action on how to actually achieve your primary goal.

It's a good example of an organized scheme to choose what and when to post. You should have a set limit on how many posts you are considering posting every day. Decide on and commit to your plan. You're going to adjust this on the go, of course, but the most important thing is to stay organized and timely.

2. Post regularly and be consistent

You will need to have a good posting strategy to keep your customers interested in your product or service. Providing daily content is a great marketing tactic as it helps keep the customers up-to-date, as well as demonstrating that you are always looking for ways to improve and add value. However, as valuable as regular content is, if you don't have a consistent approach, it will be pretty useless.

When you know exactly what your audience is asking for, the best way to provide daily content and preserve its continuity. Do your research well before you touch the Share button.

3. Approach The Social Media Channels Differently

Despite the fact that you sell the same product/service, you have to bear in mind that you do it on different social media channels. What does it mean? Which means you can't just take the posts and paste them. What's the reason? Since usually different channels mean different audiences. Many of the fans on Instagram are not members of LinkedIn and vice versa.

LinkedIn, for example, is more business-oriented and its content is a little more serious and informative than Instagram, for example, which it has users who are mostly searching for sexy and vibrant visual images.

Treat as different entities the social media channels to keep the post independent and, most importantly, exclusive. Even if you want to convey the same message, make sure that you tailor it to the different audience groups.

4. Stay engaged

Staying Engaged is all about social media. It's a method of holding the picture that your audience actually needs to see in contact, listening, and drawing. If you are not 100% committed, social media marketing is not marketing. And not only with your updates and comments, but also responding to feedback, retweeting and listening. Your clients need to know that you care for them, and if you don't get involved, well, your other tactics will be quite worthless as well.

The easiest way to communicate your dedication to the viewer is to keep them involved at all times. Ask for their opinions, create questionnaires, create unique challenges, offer rewards, discounts, etc. The secret behind every successful marketing strategy is to keep your business connected to your customers.

5. Act as a human

Acting as a human social media is all about interaction between people, not presentations and logos. When you just launch a social media marketing trip, this can be very difficult as most companies make their initial approach a hard point of sale. Avoid replacing potential and existing customers with customer reviews, product introduction, and codes of purchase. Alternatively, be as friendly as possible with your answer.

But only at the beginning do not enforce this. Your company should always find a way to behave like an individual (of course, to some extent), not to treat clients as an agency.

6. Choose Which Social Media Networks works for Your Audience

Most people worry about finding the time and energy to manage profiles on any social network. You don't have to in most situations. You just need to give the company the right social networks. You want to find out about the social networks that your intended audience is spending their time.

Next, you may need to do some research to find out where your intended audience is standing. This shouldn't be too hard, especially if you know your customers. You might be able to interview them if you don't already grasp that, asking them about their favorite social accounts.

You may start with the most popular network of your audience and then extend to include others where active social networks are run by a sufficiently large number. Nonetheless, you would not necessarily need to go beyond three or five social networks.

There we take a fairly specific definition of social networks. Clearly, in your categories you have well-known ones such as Facebook, Instagram, and Twitter. If your target audience uses them in large numbers, you could also look at video platforms such as YouTube.

7. Do not match your personal tastes with those of your target audience

The chances are that you or your company media account manager will also handle personal social pages. You have to distinguish between the two types of accounts. Just because you like to post a particular type on your own pages, it doesn't mean that those posts are going to operate on the business accounts.

You're probably posting stuff you're interested in. Nonetheless, you need to care specifically about the interests of your target audience while managing the business account. You want articles to be informative, fun, and educational.

Your specialty subjects will probably be written down. This is especially important when curating material. For example, the tweets you retweet should even be limited to those that contribute to your specific topics.

CHAPTER 9

TIPS ON HOW TO GROW YOUR PERSONAL BRAND

1. Determine what you want to be known for

Your personal brand is more than just a snapshot of who you are today; it's a guide of where to go. As well as knowing your existing skills and abilities, it is advisable to identifying your strengths and weaknesses as they apply to whatever field or profession you want to break into.

By doing so, you can reveal the strengths and attributes that make you unique, as well as the fields where you need to develop or gain new skills to succeed. Forecasting where you want to be in five to ten years— and the qualities by which you want to be known — can help you better determine what steps to take to get there.

2. Define your audience

You also need to determine who you are trying to reach before you start creating your personal brand. Is it members of the other sector? A person in a specific company? Are there recruiters? The faster you identify the target, the easier it will be to construct your narrative, because you will better understand what kind of story you need to say (and where to tell it).

3. Research your desired industry and follow the experts.

"Figure out who the thought leaders are in the area you are involved in, and not just imitate them," "Go online and find out whether they have forums or where they are sharing their opinions. Search for productive people and look at what they're doing. Imitate them, and then do better. "Your goal is to stand out in building a personal brand — but you can't get up to the top without taking stock of who's already there.

4. Embrace networking.

It is important to network frequently (and effectively) to expand your professional circle while you cultivate your ideal personal brand. Through going to formal and informal networking events, interact with colleagues and business think-leaders.

The more connections you make— and the more value you can provide in your interactions— the more likely it will be to recognize your personal brand. So, given that 85% of all positions are filled through networking, hosting such activities on a regular basis will not only help you build your business, but also theoretically advance your career.

Do not be shy about asking fellow participants to come again for an information interview or a casual coffee talk at these gatherings. And remember, if you don't have a chance to connect at the event, reach out to spark a conversation via email or LinkedIn.

5. Ask for recommendations.

You are one of the easiest and most effective ways to describe your personal brand by helping current and former employees and employers, encouraging others to express their importance to you. Just as a company might cultivate customer reviews and testimonials for use in collateral for sales and marketing, you should also cultivate your own ratings in the form of recommendations.

LinkedIn is a great place to ask for approvals as these recommendations are likely to catch the eye of future hiring managers. But don't forget to ask the people who support you to serve as a real reference during your job search, making sure they're willing to talk to a potential employer or write a letter of recommendation if necessary.

Don't you know who to ask? Former managers who directly mentored you are perfect, but other associations can also yield valuable advice, like academics and company members you belong   to.

CONCLUSION

Now that you've learned everything about marketing on social media, the next move is to build your identities and start promoting your brand online.

Just remember, it's not your magic bullet. Only if you invest time, energy, and most importantly if you reach your audience can a good marketing campaign be successful.

The social media marketing landscape may seem unpredictable, but for companies who listen, know, and want to change and adapt for successful outcomes, the outlook is certainly optimistic.

Printed in Great Britain
by Amazon